Life at the End of a Dirt Road

Chuck Nelson

PUBLISHED IN COOPERATION WITH

Stillwater Ranches

Bloomington, IN Milton Keynes, UK

authorHOUSE™

AuthorHouse™
1663 Liberty Drive, Suite 200
Bloomington, IN 47403
www.authorhouse.com
Phone: 1-800-839-8640

AuthorHouse™ UK Ltd.
500 Avebury Boulevard
Central Milton Keynes, MK9 2BE
www.authorhouse.co.uk
Phone: 08001974150

First published by AuthorHouse 6/28/2006

ISBN: 1-4259-2211-2 (sc)

Library of Congress Control Number: 2006901988

Printed in the United States of America
Bloomington, Indiana

This book is printed on acid-free paper.

FOREWORD

In the spring of 2004 we embarked on a journey to find a property of extraordinary beauty that we could protect through a conservation easement. Our travels throughout the American West didn't prepare us for the stunning vistas of the 1,700-acre Nelson Ranch. This part of the Shasta Valley has an other-worldly quality like no other place we had seen. At over 14,000 feet and perpetually snow-capped, Mount Shasta loomed over the place like something sacred, promising mystery and majesty.

In Chuck Nelson, the book's author, we found the spirit of this landscape embodied in a retired cop, dressed in Paladin black and armed with a pistol for our walks across his beloved ranch. He quickly impressed us as a sensitive, artistic and articulate man, something our stereotype of a beat cop from Oakland hadn't allowed us to anticipate. Along with his brothers Tom, David and Dan, Chuck had reluctantly decided to sell the ranch. We walked with him along the irrigation ditches, watched a golden eagle soar over Dream Point and flushed a covey of quail that Chuck knew would be just around the corner. As we watched the sunset from the top of Eagle Ridge, Chuck told us about the ancient, massive rockslide which had given birth to the landscape in front of us.

Chuck also regaled us with stories about growing up on the ranch in the 1950s and '60s. Kids today might consider it a deprived existence: no telephone, TV or indoor bathroom in the early days, chores before and after school, and learning to cope with panicky cattle, dim-witted sheep, eccentric adults and all kinds of strange, scary situations. But the ranch kid's life also included the thrills of rodeo-riding a calf, hunting snakes with a slingshot, driving a pickup at age 10 and slurping down homemade root beer and blackberry pie.

As an adult, Chuck learned to produce exceptional photographs of the ranch, as if by putting a camera up to his eye, he was transported in time to the vivid memory of his youth. He cherished visits back to the ranch as an antidote to city life, and came to treasure memories of his childhood. Despite the hardships, it made him the terrific guy he is today. Certainly it gave him courage, which served him well as a police officer for more than 30 years.

Multiple visits affirmed our decision to buy the Nelson Ranch and to learn how we could assist in the restoration of the Shasta River. We engaged California Trout and the University of California to conduct a fishery study, which demonstrated that the Nelson Ranch stretch of the Shasta River contained some of the coldest water in the Klamath Basin system and hosted a valuable nursery for endangered Coho Salmon.

This made the property extremely interesting to The Nature Conservancy. The Conservancy, a nonprofit organization dedicated to preserving biological diversity, knew that full recovery of the Shasta River as a spawning tributary to the Klamath River would be a highly desired conservation outcome. The Nature Conservancy saw an opportunity to demonstrate that modifications to traditional cattle grazing practices would return more cold water to the stream and protect this important fishery, while preserving an historic way of life. In July of 2005, with our help and the Nelsons' blessing, The Nature Conservancy proudly took title to this California treasure.

This book came to life for us around Chuck's fireplace one evening, after a steak dinner with sweet onions grown by one of Chuck's grade school chums. We were sitting around a table where, some 40 years ago, an actor and aspiring politician named Ronald Reagan had shared a similar meal and conversation. Because Chuck was concerned that his grandchildren (he calls them "grand-critters") would never understand the kind of life he led as a kid, he had begun to write down his childhood memories and adventures. He showed us the manuscript, and over the next few days we both read it, laughing out loud much of the time.

We agreed this is one of the most heart-warming, chuckle-inducing, educational and informative documents we had read in a long, long time. More than an entertaining account of Siskiyou County in the 1950s and '60s, it offers a view of an entire generation that grew up in rural America, the children of the "Greatest Generation," who learned a solid work ethic from their folks and built the strongest economy in the world.

We told Chuck that his story *had* to be published, for every kid who will never get to experience this special kind of life, and for all us grown-ups who wish we had grown up in a more innocent time, on a ranch at the end of a dirt road. In tribute to Chuck and those ranching families like the Nelsons we have come to know, we are privileged to help publish this book.

Chris Allen and Peter Adams
Stillwater Ranches

Stillwater Ranches is a company whose mission is to create profits for its investors through intelligent land investment and stewardship, combining investment goals with conservation values. **www.stillwater-ranches.com**

LIFE AT THE END OF A DIRT ROAD

Table of Contents

ACKNOWLEDGEMENTS

I would like to acknowledge my grandchildren – Ryenn, Lauren, Tawnee and Beau – for providing the spark that brought this work to life. Grandchildren inspire grandparents in many ways, but watching these special young people grow up in the city made me realize how radically different my childhood was. The contrast between their lives in the city and my experiences growing up at the end of a dirt road was my initial inspiration to put my thoughts and experiences into print.

I also want to thank my friend Joan Olsson, whose initial editing and encouragement ensured that I would complete the work. After editing an early manuscript, Joan said it made her laugh and it brought a tear to her eye. I had laughed and cried as I wrote, but until then, I had no idea I had captured those emotions in words that others could appreciate. It was Joan who first opened my eyes to the fact that "Life at the End of a Dirt Road" would appeal to a broader audience than my grandkids and immediate family.

I must especially thank Chris Allen and Peter Adams, principals of Stillwater Ranches, for their encouragement. Initially I attributed their enthusiasm to the friendship that grew out of our business relationship, or the fact that they had visited and developed a strong appreciation for the Nelson Ranch. However, when they related the positive feedback expressed by others who read their copy of the manuscript, I was reminded again of the wider audience I hope will appreciate my story. This work probably would never have been published without the strong encouragement and financial assistance of Chris and Peter.

I also need to thank Alexander ("Sandy") MacKie. Sandy was the finishing editor of this work, and his encouragement, along with his experience and wise counsel, contributed greatly to the end product.

Finally, I would like to thank my beloved wife Valerie for her patience and understanding – perhaps tolerance would be a better word. In a sense, one doesn't write a book like this, one gives birth to it. For many months she tiptoed past the door of my den while I labored over my computer, with notes and photographs strewn from floor to desktop. She provided the space and time I needed, and while I wrote, she was – as she always is – the wind beneath my wings.

INTRODUCTION

LIFE AT THE END OF A DIRT ROAD

At 3:30 in the morning, something has startled me awake. I lie there holding my breath, listening intently to the silence. The light of a full winter moon spills through the window, illuminating the covers at the foot of my bed. Then I hear it again, an unearthly wail that sounds as if it came from the pit of Hell.

As the howl trails off into a cheerless moan, I hear an excited *yip, yip, yip,* followed by another long lonesome howl. The hair on the back of my neck is standing on end. More yips and howls follow, then it's suddenly silent again. "It's just coyotes," I tell myself. "They're just dogs, wild dogs, somewhere on the hill behind the house." I look out the window and notice the junipers on Eagle Peak are casting shadows in the moonlight. Is that something moving in the shadows among the rocks and trees? I struggle to keep my 11-year-old imagination in check. "Why," I wonder, "do coyote cries make my blood run cold when they startle me awake in the middle of the night?"

On a crisp fall morning almost a year later, the country silence is broken by the familiar sounds of Canada geese in flight. Their hoarse honks grow louder as they approach, and I count seven of them flying in V-formation. I can hear the *whish, whish, whish* of their wings as they pass overhead and note the occasional tapping sound that occurs when one wingtip accidentally contacts another. They're so low I could hit them with a rock – at least that's the way a kid growing up on a ranch measures distances. They circle in front of the steep slopes of Mt. Shasta looming in the distance and lock their wings for a long, silent glide to land on the lake. What a beautiful sight – and there I am without a gun – that's the way I saw it as a kid.

The sun's heat presses against my face, and the smell of dry grass fills my nose as I set out on the type of hike a 12-year-old takes when he needs to be out and about but has no particular destination in mind. It's quiet but not silent as I pick my path between the rocks and sagebrush on Indian Hill. Birds provide background music while my boots clunk against the rocks and sagebrush whisks against my blue jeans. Occasionally there's the sound of a grasshopper fleeing my clumsy path or a cow mooing to her calf in a distant field. A hawk circling high overhead adds its occasional scream to round out the sounds of a summer day on the ranch.

Then there's an instantly recognizable *shuka, shuka* sound at my feet. A rattlesnake is letting me know he's there, and I'm too close. I'm airborne in an instant – trying to keep up with my heart that jumped ahead of me. By the time I land a few feet away, my eyes have found the snake coiled under sagebrush next to my path. I look all around to see if there's another. They sometimes come in pairs. Finding none, I quickly gather some rocks and throw them at the snake. The snake's *shuka, shuka* warning rattle turns to an angry *buzz*. I figure there's no shortage of rattlesnakes on the ranch, and one less will make my hikes safer. When the snake is dead, I take out my pocketknife and cut off the rattles. They will be my trophy. With my heart back in my chest and my trophy in my shirt pocket, I resume the hike to the tune of clunking boots, birds and grasshoppers. Behind me, the hawk calls again, and I wonder if its family will be having snake on their menu tonight.

Have you ever wondered what it would be like growing up on a cattle ranch? Most people grow up in a small town, suburban or urban environment, so they can only imagine it. I had the unusual experience and advantage of growing up deep in the country. My ranch experience represents a thin slice of the Americana pie, but it's a rich portion and worth sharing with others who might appreciate a taste of something different.

In the following pages you'll get a look at life through the eyes of a kid growing up on a cattle ranch in Siskiyou County, California, in the mid-20th century. Kids don't see things the way adults do, so for much of this book I'll be putting my adult self out to pasture and giving you a kid's perspective. You'll probably find him more interesting than his grown-up version anyway.

Everything recorded here is based on true events and experiences, but you will have to allow some room for the kid's imagination. I should warn you that the kid who grew up on the ranch wasn't always wise or kind, and often failed to properly respect and appreciate the natural wonders he enjoyed. I make no defense for him except to note that his conduct was typical of his age and generation. In truth he loved the ranch and the wildlife that came with it, but he was often a bit hard on the flora and fauna as well as pets and little brothers. He had a tendency to see creatures as targets, rather than to appreciate them as works of creation. He was just a kid, so I ask your indulgence. He knows better now.

To get an authentic feeling for ranch life, you'd have to get dust in your nose, step in a cowpie, dodge a few snakes, get splinters in your hands and be skeeter-bit every day for at least a month. You'd have to do outside chores before sunrise and after sunset, and before and after school every day. On weekends you would have extra chores, but you'd still have time for fishing or hunting. You'd have to work outside when it's too hot and when it's too cold; when it's raining or snowing. You would have to chop wood for the stove to get warm on a winter morning. You'd have to get hay stickers down your neck, while sweat streaks through the dust on your face. You'd learn to listen to country silence until you can actually hear it. You would experience the serenity of isolation without being lonely. When you'd experienced or imagined all of these things, then you'd *begin* to know what it's like growing up on a ranch. It's not always easy but it is not at all bad, just different, a rare privilege that few experience.

From the perspective of a youngster growing up on a cattle ranch, life in the city seemed foreign and forbidding. All of those noises, houses, cars and people were intimidating. From what I could hear over the radio or read in the newspaper, the city was a place where bad news occurred. It was a place where there were terrible accidents, horrendous crimes, catastrophic fires and dangerous riots. Cities were the habitat of undesirable people such as burglars, scam artists, lawyers and politicians. I couldn't imagine why anybody would ever want to live in a place like that.

Infrequent visits to the city with my parents did nothing to change my opinion. Urban lights and noises were harsh and unfamiliar. It was exciting but disturbing at the same time. City folk always seemed in a hurry, and it was astounding to see so many people with so many places to go. I felt out of place and in the way in the city. I was always more comfortable back on the ranch. OK, you could say I was more at home on the range.

As I got older, I began to realize how fortunate I was to live on a ranch. I really had the best deal going. When friends and relatives who lived in the city visited the ranch, I was able to see the ranch through their eyes. They marveled over the simplest things and were scared of everything from guns to bugs, snakes, cattle and coyotes. They seemed to be learning for the first time where hay, eggs, meat and milk come from. All of this affirmed my opinion that I had an advantage over folks who lived in the city. Growing up on a ranch was the best possible life – at least it was for me. I'm still convinced of that but perhaps not for all the same reasons.

Living on a ranch gives one a perspective about life, death and nature that can't be obtained in the city. My experience was unusual, not just because I was raised on a ranch but because I grew up without telephone or television. These technologies were available during my childhood, but they had not yet found their way into the nooks and crannies of rural America. We were exposed to modern technology, but not influenced by it to the extent that urban America was. Whether this was an advantage or a disadvantage, I have not yet decided. I am convinced that if it was a disadvantage, it was a small one.

It's ironic that the kid who never wanted to live in the city ended up being a big-city cop. I guess it's just one of life's mysteries. I'm writing this as a retired cop looking back through 34 years of mostly municipal law enforcement to recall a childhood lived at the end of a dirt road in another age, in another world. I have experienced the best and worst of both ranch and city life, and I admit that it is sometimes more pleasant to look back on life as a ranch kid than as a beat cop. I have the advantage of having experienced both lifestyles and the perspective that comes with that combination.

This book is not a scholarly documentary; it's just me trying to recall and share what I saw, felt, thought and did as a kid growing up on a ranch. The narrative won't flow in a chronological sequence with a clear beginning, middle and end. If this work were compared to a meal, it wouldn't be a formal meal that starts with appetizers followed by salad, main course then dessert. It would be more like a pizza – you get a little bit of everything with every bite. To get all the flavor or to see the big picture, you will have to read all the chapters then step back, digest them and squint your eyes until you "see" what ranch life was like back then. Best of all, as a literary pizza, it won't give you gas.

A sense of humor has been an important survival tool for me through the years. Whether I was stepping in a cowpie or investigating a murder, I found it useful to find a light side to help me deal with it. A bit of humor may show up from time to time as we roll up our sleeves, get dusty and explore life at the end of a dirt road through the eyes of a kid who was there.

CHAPTER ONE

THE SETTING

It was very near Christmas in 1947 when the Nelsons moved onto the property that was to become known as the Nelson Ranch. My father, Sedgley ("Sedg"), worked for the University of California Agricultural Extension Service as a Farm Advisor and had recently been assigned to Siskiyou County. He had graduated from the University of California at Davis with a degree in agriculture and made his living promoting agriculture and providing technical advice for farmers and ranchers. Owning and operating his own ranch had been his dream for many years. My mother, Elsie, had been raised in North-Central California and was immersed in farming and agriculture all of her life. Purchasing the ranch was a dream come true for both of them.

Along with the rest of the nation, my parents had weathered the Depression and had just come through the war years. My father had served as a pilot and flight trainer in the Army Air Corps, but the war ended just before he was sent overseas. Now they were hoping to settle down into a normal life where they could turn their dreams into reality. My older brother Tom, born in 1942, and I (1944) were their only children at the time. Tom was 5 ½ years old, and I was 3 ½ when we made the move that changed all of our lives forever. Two more brothers joined the family later, David (1949) and Dan (1954).

MT. SHASTA LOOMS AHEAD WHEN YOU DRIVE THE DUSTY ROAD TO THE RIVER.

The Nelson Ranch is located in the Big Springs community of the Shasta Valley in Northern California. The ranch house sits at the end of a dirt road that winds its way among juniper-covered volcanic hills. The hills are a prominent feature of the ranch and dominate much of the western portion of Shasta Valley.

The story of how the ranch's hilly landscape came violently into existence is a fascinating tale of geologic catastrophism. I could just tell you that the hills on our ranch fell off of Mt. Shasta, but that explanation leaves a few loose ends and isn't particularly satisfying. The real story involves a geologic event on a scale that boggles the imagination. If I had known the true story when I was a kid, I would have been very reluctant to turn my back on Mt. Shasta while growing up in its shadow.

Please bear with me in this chapter as I wax a bit technical to describe the geologic history and the flora and fauna of the ranch. This sets the stage for the rest of the book, the mostly non-technical story of a boy who grew up atop this awesome avalanche.

Much of our landscape, including the hills, was once part of a slightly larger ancestral Mt. Shasta that stood some 15 miles south and east of the ranch, where the modern Mt. Shasta stands today. The ancient Mt. Shasta was unstable, and at some point in the distant past a major portion of the mountain broke away and plummeted into the Shasta Valley as a massive debris avalanche. Geologists have estimated that this prehistoric avalanche deposited more than 10 cubic miles of material over some 260 square miles.

The hills that cover much of the Nelson Ranch and a good portion of the western side of the Shasta Valley were once huge chunks of rock (block facies) and unconsolidated deposits of volcaniclastic material (pyroclastic flows, lahars, air fall tephra and alluvium) that were originally deposited on the slopes of the ancestral Mt. Shasta.

Geologists believe the avalanche occurred during the Pleistocene Epoch some 300,000 years ago. The so-called Ice Age is associated with the Pleistocene, so it may be that large quantities of snow and ice accumulated on the upper regions of the mountain, contributing to its instability. When some geologic force triggered the avalanche, huge units of rock and unconsolidated volcanic material, mixed with snow, glacial ice and groundwater, broke loose from the northwestern flank of the volcanic cone and hurtled downhill in a colossal avalanche.

The avalanche transported and deposited huge block facies (today's hills) over a 30-mile stretch extending north from Mt. Shasta to the present town of Montague. The hills become progressively smaller toward the northern boundary of the avalanche path, indicating that the block facies broke into smaller pieces (disaggregated) as they were carried along in the debris flow.

During the avalanche, the block facies were immersed in a water-saturated, unsorted mudflow-like matrix of sand, silt, clay and rock fragments. Most of the debris in the mudflow (matrix facies) was derived from the ancestral Mt. Shasta, but the avalanche picked up and incorporated non-volcanic rock, debris and additional water along the way.

After the avalanche came to rest, the liquid portion of the matrix facies drained away down the Shasta and Klamath River valleys, leaving much of the western portion of the Shasta Valley covered with a mix of unsorted and unstratified silt, sand, pebbles, cobbles and boulders. This residual matrix facies still covers the tops and sides of most of the hills as well as the flat areas between hills. In many locations on the ranch, the matrix facies formed something we called *hardpan,* a consolidated mix of silt, sand and rock that's almost as hard as cement. The hardpan is so dense in some places that we had to use dynamite to dig postholes for fences.

LOOKING SOUTH FROM EAGLE PEAK ACROSS THE LAKE TOWARD MT. SHASTA, A NUMBER OF HILLS (INCLUDING EAGLE PEAK) CAN BE SEEN AS THE REMNANTS OF AN ANCIENT DEBRIS AVALANCHE THAT SLIPPED FROM THE NORTHWESTERN SLOPES OF AN ANCIENT MT. SHASTA AND TUMBLED INTO THE WESTERN PORTION OF THE SHASTA VALLEY.

It's amazing to consider that the hills that give our ranch privacy and character were once huge chunks of andesite rock deposited on the distant slopes of an ancestral Mt. Shasta. Not only did Mt. Shasta give us a most favorable view, it gave us our very landscape. Can you imagine what it must have looked and sounded like when the massive debris avalanche hurtled through the area?

The Nelson Ranch is located near the middle of the debris avalanche, so it's no surprise that the terrain is rocky. When a flat area between the hills is developed for agricultural use, it must first be cleared of rocks, rocks and more rocks. Through the years we hauled many loads of rock ourselves, and large rock piles beyond the edges of the irrigated pastures indicated others had done the same before us. A number of rock fences around the ranch showed that previous generations of ranchers had taken advantage of the ranch's most plentiful natural resource, lava rock, to mark property lines and keep their livestock from straying.

> **More about the Avalanche**
>
> The fascinating story of the debris avalanche that covers the Nelson Ranch and much of the western portion of the Shasta Valley can be found in USGS Survey Bulletin 1861 titled, *Gigantic Debris Avalanche of Pleistocene Age From Ancestral Mount Shasta Volcano, California and Debris-Avalanche Hazard Zonation.* (After reading the title, you might think it unnecessary to read the rest of the report, but I assure you that it contains many interesting details that didn't make it into the title.) The report was written by Dwight Crandell and published in 1989.

Over time, our family gave each major hill on the ranch a name. Naming the hills made it easier to give directions and describe locations, but it also tied a bit of history to the land. Eagle Peak, the rocky prominence behind the ranch house, was named for an eagle sighting in the early years on the ranch. At the foot of Salvadori Hill (which was named after the man who sold the ranch to my parents) sat the remains of the old Salvadori homestead. Dream Point was named for its view. It's a place where you can sit and dream about building a house with a view that stretches to the horizon in every direction. Chuck Buck Hill was named by my father because I killed a deer there when I was a kid. Government Hill was owned by the federal government until my father bought it and added it to the ranch. I named Mummy Hill after a bad dream in which I imagined mummies marching down the slopes. My brother Tom named the hill across the lake from the house Indian Hill. He said he christened it Indian Hill for no particular reason other than wanting to put his stamp on a hill before I named them all.

The ranch landscape is dotted with juniper trees and sagebrush. Bronco grass fills much of the open space between the rocks and trees. The ubiquitous bronco grass provides range feed for cattle and sports seasonal colors of green, maroon and brown. It nods in deference to the slightest breeze, and you can trace a gust of wind across a hillside by watching the ripples in the bronco grass. Known also as cheatgrass or Mormon oats, bronco grass is a native of the Mediterranean area introduced to the Northwest in the late 1800s. It's a hardy plant that thrives under harsh conditions, and it's present today in much of the Northwestern United States. Since it overtakes many native plants, some consider it a weed, but I always took it for granted as a familiar part of the ranch's high desert landscape.

Sagebrush is also plentiful on the ranch and adds touches of gray, green and blue

A SAGEBRUSH GOING TO SEED IN THE FALL.

to the color palette. When in bloom, the sagebrush (also known as rabbit brush) sports yellow flowering tips that turn to fluffy seedpods in the fall. The juniper trees are dark green with a tint of gray. Juniper berries are blue-gray and taste really bad. At one time or another, and whether on purpose or by accident, a kid is bound to taste everything on the ranch.

BLUE-GRAY BERRIES ADORN THE LIMBS OF A JUNIPER TREE.

During the summer months, a trip down the dirt road leading to the ranch produces a billowing cloud of light brown dust that always manages to fill the car, not to mention your eyes, nose, hair and clothing. If you live on a ranch, you have to learn to live with dust. The dust cloud trailing behind a car makes it extremely important to be in the first car if two or more cars are entering the ranch at the same time, to avoid being enveloped in dust raised by the lead car.

When more than one car enters the ranch at the same time, etiquette dictates that the lead car should drive slowly to minimize the dust, and good sense dictates that the following cars hold back until some of the dust has settled and you can actually see where you're going. You soon adjust to living with dust, and it was my observation as a youth that a wet comb and a bit of dust in your hair would form a "glue" that worked as well or better than that green stuff in which we used to dip our combs to corral our cowlicks.

In the winter months, rain and snow replace the dust with mud. When you live on a ranch, you also have to learn to live with mud. For most of the winter the road is either muddy and slippery or frozen rock-hard. In the early years, before the road was improved, deep ruts would form during the winter. When the ruts froze solid, we could take our hands off the steering wheel and the car would stay on the road, steering itself with its wheels locked in the frozen ruts.

DUSTY ROADS TURN TO MUD IN THE WINTER.

It's about a mile from the ranch house to the paved county road that links the ranch to civilization. In Siskiyou County, civilization consists of scattered ranches and an occasional town. The dirt road leading to the ranch eventually was officially named Nelson Road. The paved county road was originally called the 99-97 Cut Off because it cut across the Shasta Valley connecting the old Highway 99 (now Interstate 5) with Highway 97. Today, the 99-97 Cut Off is known as County Road A-12.

From where Nelson Road connects with County Road A-12, it's about five miles to the closest town, Grenada. Somehow that distance from civilization always seemed just about right. Upon our arrival in Siskiyou County, the town of Grenada consisted of 300 people, but it had a bar (The Cattleman's Club), a general store (The Grenada Mercantile), a barbershop (off and on) and a post office (off and on). It also had a Texaco gas station, a feed and grain store, and the elementary school we attended.

Another 10 miles up the road from Grenada, about 15 miles from the ranch, is Yreka, the County Seat. When we moved to Siskiyou County, Yreka had a population of around 4,000 to 5,000. It had a couple of grocery stores, drug stores, appliance stores, a Penny's, a movie theater, several bars, a hotel and a few motels. Yreka even had a bakery or two.

I remember looking out through the window from inside the Yreka Bakery on Miner Street and noticing that the letters "YREKA BAKERY" were backwards but still spelled "YREKA BAKERY." In later life I learned that when a word or phrase spells the same thing forward and backward (like "yo, banana boy" or "race car"), it's called a palindrome. As a kid, encountering a palindrome was mildly interesting but not as captivating as the aromas from the sweet pastries that filled glass cases in the bakery. We attended high school and did most of our major grocery shopping in Yreka, which was as close to a city as we normally came.

The Nelson Ranch sits at an elevation of about 2,500 feet toward the center of the Shasta Valley, a depression between the Cascade Mountains on the east and the Klamath Mountains on the west. With the Siskiyou Mountains to the north and the Eddys, Scott and Trinity Mountains to the south, the valley is rimmed with peaks that stand tall and blue against the horizon in every direction. Mt. Shasta, a 14,162-foot snow-capped volcano, stands about 15 miles from the ranch at the southeast end of the valley. It's the unrivaled aesthetic centerpiece for the entire valley as well as the ranch. With constantly changing atmospheric and lighting conditions, Shasta seems like a different mountain each time you look at it. The mountain is a majestic presence, a silent sentinel keeping watch over the ranch and the Shasta Valley.

A STEEL SKY AND WHITE MOUNTAIN RISE ABOVE THE LAKE IN AUTUMN.

The ranch consists of 1,704 acres, including a lake and a stretch of the

Shasta River that meanders for nearly five miles along the south and west borders. The lake is about 40 acres in size but has no outlet, so it tends to be stagnant and saturated with alkali from the surrounding volcanic soil. Mom didn't want us to swim in it, but the mud, smell and algae were even more convincing than her instructions. The lake is too stagnant and alkaline for fish, but ducks and mud hens love it, so the lake is always dotted with waterfowl. We often joked that the lake was too thick to drink and too thin to plow, but the cattle drank the lake water with no ill effects. Blackbirds fill the tules along the shore each spring, and during the winter Canada geese and swans frequently visit. Abundant killdeer and other shore birds add their calls to the daily sounds of the lake.

The river is always good for fishing, and it adds a refreshing green riparian strip to what is otherwise high desert countryside. The river water is a bit cool but otherwise good for swimming if you don't mind mud, moss and mosquitoes and can cope with the fear of stepping on a crawdad.

While most of the ranch consists of rocky hills and rangeland, it eventually came to include over 200 acres of pasture. Most of those 200 acres are irrigated by water pumped from the Shasta River, but in later years, some fields were irrigated with well water. River water is superior to the well water because the mineral content of most wells in the Big Springs area is pretty high, and sometimes it can be hard on things that like to grow. Some of the water in the area was so hard that neighbors said you had to chew it a while before you could swallow it. Ours wasn't that bad. We were raised on ranch well water, and it did us no harm. I have always liked water with a bit of flavor.

Wildlife was always abundant on the ranch. The ranch house was a man-made island in the midst of wild country that began at our front and back doors. At one time or another, I have seen jack rabbits and cottontail rabbits, deer, coyotes, kangaroo mice, pack rats, badgers, weasels, squirrels, rock chucks, bobcats, mountain lions, gophers, moles, field mice, raccoons, porcupines, beaver, muskrats, otters and other critters that I have forgotten. By way of reptiles, we had rattlesnakes, gopher snakes, water snakes, king snakes, turtles and blue belly lizards. Resident amphibians included assorted frogs and toads. The river also contained clams, hellgrammites and crawdads, not to mention fish of various types. Birds of every sort were in abundance: meadowlarks, killdeer, robins, blackbirds, quail, pheasants, ducks, swans, geese, sparrows, finches, magpies, woodpeckers, flickers, herons, cranes, egrets, hawks, eagles, buzzards and many others.

Part of growing up on the ranch is learning to identify the common name for each creature we saw with any regularity. As a kid, I took all of this wildlife for granted because it was always there around me. When I went for a hike, I expected to see and hear wildlife. I wondered why visitors from the city got so excited about seeing something that I lived with every day.

Wildlife is something that we hear as much as see. Today as an adult I love to hear the sounds, especially the birdcalls that came from sources invisible to me as a kid. The sounds of the birds and animals that I took for granted on the ranch must have been imprinted in my subconscious, as it's a special treat when I hear them today. I believe a meadowlark can pack into a four-second trill what it takes a symphony orchestra 20 minutes to unpack. The seats are cheaper too if you don't mind a few mosquitoes, ticks and snakes.

When I hear a meadowlark today, I'm transported to a spring day on the ranch. A killdeer call brings the smell of the lake to my nose and memories of hot summer days to my mind. The memory of coyotes howling at 4:00 in the morning still sends chills down my spine. When I hear certain wildlife sounds today, it stirs something deep inside of me in the same way that listening to "oldies" on the radio stirs memories of bygone years. It is a form of music that links me to my experiences on a ranch at the end of a dirt road.

L/R: MAGPIE, DAVID, CHUCK, DAN. DAVID IS CRINGING BECAUSE THE MAGPIE HAS EITHER DUG ITS TALONS INTO THE TOP OF HIS HEAD OR POOPED DOWN THE BACK OF HIS NECK.

Today, when the background noise of the city dims to the point that I can hear a magpie, I'm flooded with magpie memories. As a kid, we had magpie pets that we taught to talk just as you would a parrot. Magpies are noisy birds, but they have great personalities and make wonderful pets. Elmer, Joe and Magee were my favorites.

A baby magpie squawks loudly when being fed, and a nest full of baby magpies raises a commotion that can be heard for some distance. In the early spring, I would follow the magpie racket to its source in a pile of sticks high in a juniper tree. I'd climb the tree and select my pet from among the siblings. The mother magpie never seemed to notice that she had one less beak to feed, and the baby magpie took me on as a substitute "mom" as soon as I fed it. I fed my magpies bread dipped in milk, raw hamburger and the occasional grasshopper or locust.

We kept them in a cage when they were young, but as they got older, by accident or by design, they eventually got loose. They love to land on top of your head, which they apparently consider to be as dead as a stump because they dig their claws in to keep from falling off. To show their affection they will "talk" gibberish to you while pecking the top of your head and pooping down your back. Magpies make great pets but not when you're wearing your good clothes.

Summers on the ranch were hot, and it was common to swelter through temperatures over 100° for several days in a row. Since the ranch was situated in high desert terrain, annual rainfall was only about 10 inches. On hot summer days, the heat sometimes chased the wind, creating dust devils that swirled dust and grass and sometimes lifted tumbleweeds into the air. As kids we chased the dust devils and tried to stand in the center of the swirling dust and debris. It filled our eyes, ears, noses, hair and clothes with dirt, but it always seemed like a good idea at the time. Summer also brings thunderstorms. Thunderheads tower over the valley, and there's nothing as refreshing as the smell of ozone and the feel of ice-cold raindrops or hail to cool down a hot summer day.

Winter was as cold as summer was hot. Sometimes the temperature stayed below freezing for a few weeks, and the lake froze over. With a good solid freeze we could walk all over the lake. Winter in Siskiyou County also brings bitter, strong winds. I can remember the wind's blowing for days. At night powerful gusts howled and shrieked, making the juniper trees sway and hiss. I vividly recall lying in my bed and listening to the wind as it whistled, moaned and tore angrily at the corners of the house.

We usually got several snows during the winter. Typical snowfalls were 2 to 6 inches, but we sometimes had deposits over a foot deep. In the early days after a good snow, the folks sometimes pulled Tom or me on a sled behind the car when they drove the mile from the ranch to the county road to collect the mail. The mailbox was out at the county road, and when my father was away on his frequent business trips or couldn't pick up the mail on his way home from work, someone else made the mail run.

DEEP TRACKS ARE LEFT IN THE SNOW AND MUD WHEN THE PICKUP HAULS HAY TO HUNGRY CATTLE DURING A WINTER FEEDING.

It was always a treat to wake up in the morning and look out my window to find an unexpected snow-covered world. There's something special about a hike in the country during a snowstorm or after a fresh snow. It's as though you are the first and only person in a new, unexplored country where the only footprints to be found are your own. Sometimes a cold fog closed us in for a week or more at a time. The cold winter fog would snake through the junipers and freeze on the trees, grass and barbed wire fences, coating everything with a white, hoary frost.

Every season has its own character, and you could decide for yourself whether it was something beautiful or a hardship. Sometimes it seemed too hot, and other times it seemed too cold. It was too windy, too dusty or too something much of the time. When we complained about the weather, my father would say, "As a rule, a man's a fool; when it's hot, he wants it cool. When it's cool, he wants it hot, always wanting what it's not." To avoid repetition of this annoying recitation, we learned to endure and even enjoy what we couldn't change.

NELSON RANCH IN THE SHASTA VALLEY

A catastrophic avalanche from an ancestral Mt. Shasta created the rocky hills that characterize the western regions of the Shasta Valley.

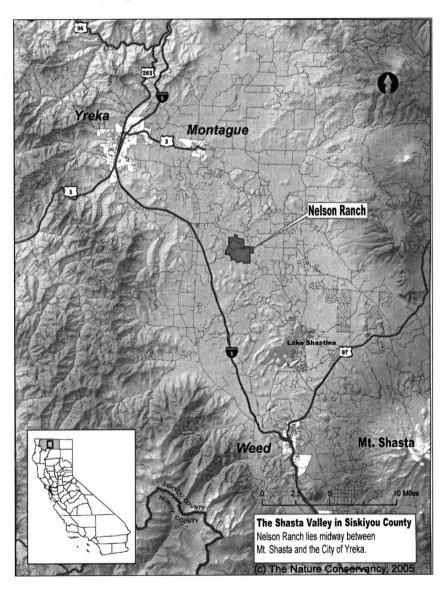

The Shasta Valley in Siskiyou County
Nelson Ranch lies midway between Mt. Shasta and the City of Yreka.

(c) The Nature Conservancy, 2005

MAP OF THE NELSON RANCH

Purchased by Sedg and Elsie Nelson in 1947, the Nelson Ranch was acquired by The Nature Conservancy in 2005.

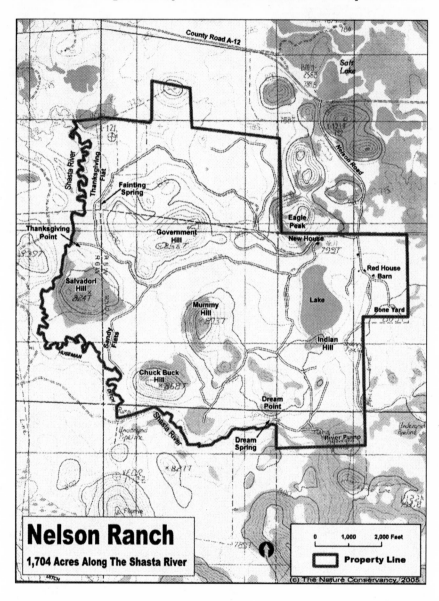

Nelson Ranch

1,704 Acres Along The Shasta River

CHAPTER TWO

THE RED HOUSE

In 1947 my parents bought what would become the Nelson Ranch from a colorful Siskiyou County character by the name of Angelo Salvadori.

When we moved onto the ranch, we found ourselves in what could be characterized as an exceptionally rustic ranch house, what a realtor today would probably call a great "fixer-upper."

As soon as we moved in, my father and mother began to fix it up by adding mod-

L/R: CHUCK, SEDG & TOM OUTSIDE THE BACK PORCH OF THE RED HOUSE BEFORE IT WAS RED.

ern amenities such as linoleum and an indoor bathroom. With extra boards over the cracks in the walls to keep the wind out during the winter and the flies out during the summer, and with drywall on the inside walls, it soon became reasonably comfortable.

The house had been whitewashed at some time in the distant past, but my father painted it red, and it became the Red House that we knew and loved.

There were a number of stories, or perhaps legends, told about Mr. Salvadori. He was reported to be a man of exceptional strength who had once won a bet by lifting and carrying a waterlogged telephone pole to demonstrate his power. It was also said that he ran a moonshine still on the ranch in cooperation with the local sheriff. There may be some truth to this story; an old home site on what we called Salvadori Hill was littered with coiled tubing, barrel hoops and other paraphernalia consistent with operating a still.

According to another story, Mrs. Salvadori hauled the furniture out of the house on Salvadori Hill and burned it to the ground because she wanted a better house. She apparently had a will of her own, was not given to subtlety and knew how to motivate her husband. She couldn't have been too picky when it came to houses because our Red House was the "better" new house.

When we first moved into the Red House, the yard was distinguished by an extraordinary collection of litter and garbage. The greatest concentrations had accumulated at throwing distance from the front and back doors.

Ranchers are notorious for saving every scrap of wood or metal because they never know when they might need that very thing to complete a project around the ranch. The previous owners had taken this concept to the extreme. To the uninformed, the place might have looked like a junkyard, but the experienced rancher realizes that an old catsup bottle, tin can or rusted-out coffee pot might come in handy some day. My folks must have been among the uninformed because they spent several days hauling the junk away. Fortunately, in those days, the local dump was only about three miles away, just off of the county road as you headed toward Grenada.

The Red House was quite small, but it had a kitchen, a living room and a den that adjoined the bathroom, which was also the laundry room. Off the living room was a master bedroom that you walked through to get to the back (kids') bedroom. Under the back end of the house was a hand-dug cellar that was entered from outside the house through an attached storage shed. On the east side of the house a screened-in back porch was used to store our winter supply of wood for the kitchen stove and fireplace.

One of the first challenges my folks faced was to convince the chickens, horse, goats and other animals that they were no longer welcomed guests *inside* the house. My first memory of the ranch was visiting it with my father before we moved onto the place. While I was only about 3-1/2 years old, I remember thinking how cool it was to have all these animals wandering through the house. I recall a pony in the kitchen, chickens coming and going through the back door, which stood open, and a goat standing in a red stuffed armchair eating ashes out of an ashtray. While my dad talked with Mr. Salvadori, I ducked the flies that were bouncing off the windows and watched the animals come and go. First impressions are important and, and as far as I could see, this was a really neat place!

My folks didn't share my opinion about ranch animals in the house and established new rules. After evicting the dismayed animals, my parents scraped their deposits off the floor and scrubbed it really well – several times. But the oiled wood floor still smelled like manure, and my father laid linoleum to provide a clean surface and to cover the source of odor.

THE OUTHOUSE

When we first moved into the Red House, it didn't have an indoor bathroom. We used an outhouse that was about 75 feet across the road. The outhouse rivaled the dank cellar as a scary place. Not only were there spiders to be concerned about, but the outhouse's dark holes looked and smelled like they led to the end of the world, if not the very pit of Hell.

Although only one person used it at a time, the outhouse was a two-holer. I always worried about falling through. Just to be safe, I'd brace myself well when using the facility. Anything could be down there.

The worst time to use the outhouse was at night because when you step out of the house on a moonless night in the country, it's pitch black. There are no streetlights, no ambient city light. It's just country dark. A moonless country night reveals a beautiful inky black sky full of brilliant stars shining down at you. For a kid with an over-active imagination, it wasn't so much beautiful as it was spooky. Stepping out the door into the black of night with nothing but a flashlight to keep the snakes, spiders, coyotes, dragons and monsters away was a scary experience.

Imagine trying to hold onto the flashlight while taking care of business and properly bracing yourself so you don't fall into the stinking abyss, and you can see what kind of a predicament a late-night visit to the outhouse was. Sometimes when the coyotes had been howling a lot, Mom would accompany me and wait outside with a lantern while I used the facilities. The only good thing about the experience was that we had real toilet paper rather than a Sears and Roebuck catalog.

I will always remember what it was like to step out of the warmth of the Red House into a bitter winter night to walk through utter darkness to that scary outhouse. With that experience as an incentive, Dad worked hard to get us an indoor toilet. When it arrived, it was ever so welcomed.

While the indoor bathroom was greatly appreciated, the location of the kids' bedroom at the back of the house presented a logistics problem for me. If I had to use the bathroom in the middle of the night, I had to walk from the back bedroom through a short hallway, my parents' bedroom, the living room and the den to get to the bathroom. This was a bit of an obstacle course in the dark but not insurmountable.

My problem was twofold – in addition to being afraid of the dark, I had to contend with my father grinding his teeth in his sleep. This was a bad combination for a little kid with a big imagination. I would lie in bed, desperately in need of relief, but I kept hearing a "grrraack, grrraaack, grrraack" sound coming from the darkness beyond the hallway. As near as I could figure, this was precisely the sound an alligator would make. This meant that there must be a huge alligator lurking in the darkness somewhere between me and the bathroom.

Given the option of wetting the bed or approaching an alligator-infested room, I did what any reasonable kid would do. In the morning I would get in trouble for wetting the bed, and my mother would again explain that the noise in the night was only my father grinding his teeth. But this didn't fool me. I knew better. I had tried to duplicate the sound by grinding my own teeth and couldn't do it. Besides, I knew an alligator when I heard one.

THE FIREPLACE

Apart from a couple of electric heaters and a wood stove in the kitchen, there was no heat in the Red House. On cold winter mornings, Tom and I would climb out of bed, grab our clothes and run across ice-cold floors into the kitchen to get dressed in front of the wood-burning stove. In the process, we managed to burn ourselves in both public and private places with some regularity.

In order to improve the heating situation, my folks decided to have a fireplace built out of lava rocks that were in abundant supply within a few steps in any direction. Dad collected a large pile in front of the house and we were ready for construction to begin. To build the fireplace, my parents hired a gnarly old codger with hair protruding in many directions from various surfaces and orifices.

I don't know what he charged for the job, but part of the deal included a fifth of whiskey a day, which he consumed as he worked. Mom went to great lengths to keep Tom and me away from him, "so the man can work." Whiskey notwithstanding, he built a fine fireplace that will undoubtedly outlast the house. I imagine that when the codger died, his family saved a lot of money on funeral expenses because he should have been pretty well embalmed by then.

The fireplace quickly replaced the kitchen stove as our dressing room heater. Tom and I soon learned to hold our pants in front of the crackling fire until they were toasty and enjoyed the unsurpassed luxury of pulling on a warm pair of pants on a cold winter morning.

When you don't have television, much of family life is spent reading or relaxing in the warmth of a fireplace. Sometimes we just sat and talked, or listened to the radio while gazing into the flickering flames and glowing coals. On occasion we roasted wieners or toasted marshmallows in the fireplace. When the power went out, my mother cooked over the fireplace. A fireplace can be something of a family entertainment center at the end of a dirt road.

THE CELLAR

The hand-dug cellar was a particularly spooky place for me as a kid. It was a dark, cold pit under the floor of the attached storage shed where Mom stored canned food. Mom preserved a lot of food in glass jars but, for reasons I never figured out, she called it *canning* rather than *jarring*. At the end of summer, the cellar shelves were lined with jars of fruits, vegetables and jams.

I dreaded the occasions when my mother sent me to the cellar to fetch a jar of jelly. To get to the cellar, I had to exit the house and enter the storage shed at the back of the house, a particularly spooky trip on cold, windy nights. The storage shed was a favorite habitat of some of the ugliest spiders I had ever seen, and I have never developed an appreciation for creatures with more than four legs. To make things worse, the shed had a squeaky door and a creaky wooden floor.

STAIRWAY DESCENDING INTO THE DREADED CELLAR.

When the wind was howling, the walls creaked, moaned and hissed.

As I entered the shed, a heavy trap door lay on the floor in front of me. I often imagined how awful it would be if I were to step on that trap door and it gave way, sending me plunging into the dank darkness of the dreaded cellar. To open the trapdoor, I had to pull really hard on a cable that dangled next to the wall. The cable went up through a couple of pulleys and back down to attach to a heavy iron ring on the trapdoor. When I pulled the cable, the pulleys and hinges squeaked and groaned as the trapdoor slowly lifted. In the dim light I could see the top steps of a steep wooden stairway leading into the black abyss below. I knew what horrors could be awaiting me down there.

A string dangling from the ceiling of the storage shed turned on a single light bulb, which only managed to illuminate the first few steps leading to the cellar. I would work my way down the steep steps slowly, letting my eyes adjust to the darkness and making sure not to touch anything in case there was a spider waiting to jump on me. The farther down the steps I went, the colder it became, and the danker and mustier the air smelled. As I inched my way down the steps, I could feel the cold cellar air surround my body: first my ankles, then my legs, then my arms and finally my head. It was as if I being immersed in invisible water.

The cellar floor and walls were dirt and rock, and the smell of damp dirt filled the air. In the middle of the cellar, a string dangled from a single light bulb. It was too dark to see the string, so I had to wave my hand frantically above my head to locate it, all the while hoping I wouldn't grab a huge spider that I knew was dangling above. When I finally found the string and gave it a pull, it lit the most pathetic light bulb I ever saw. The weak light pushed away only a few feet of the encroaching darkness, leaving all too many corners and nooks as dark as ever. Anything could be hiding in those places: a snake, a crazed and starved coyote, or a mountain lion. We didn't have bear on the ranch, but if we did, this is undoubtedly where they would hang out.

Finally, as my eyes adjusted, I could see dark objects lining the wooden shelves against the wall. One of these must be the jar of blackberry jam I had been sent to retrieve. The trick was to grab one that didn't have a spider on it then get out of there before something really bad emerged from the dark corners of the cellar. Taking my best shot at a "spider-free" jar, I grabbed one and raced up the stairs. As I climbed toward the light and warmth above, I examined the jar for spider attachments. At the top of the stairs I pushed the trapdoor shut and stomped on it for good measure. After fighting the wind to close and bolt the door, I would dash for the house. I had survived another trip into the horrifying pit we called the cellar.

When I triumphantly presented the jar of jam to Mom, she would ask, "Did you turn out the light in the cellar?" My answer was always, "Yes!" I figured I could turn it out next time I was down there or possibly blame it on Tom. In any event I wasn't about to tempt fate twice in the same day.

CRITTERS

Country life in general and ranch life in particular involves raising critters. In the fields, barns and sheds near the ranch house, we at one time or another raised milk cows, horses, chickens, pigs, sheep, goats, ducks, turkeys and rabbits.

Chickens were an important part of our home operation because they supplied both eggs and meat.

CHUCK, SHEP & SHEEP. IT'S DIFFICULT TO BE LONELY WHEN SURROUNDED BY FRIENDS.

We always had plenty of eggs and often enjoyed fried chicken. Mom could cook a chicken dinner from hatchet to skillet in one day. When we killed a tough old hen, Mom made chicken croquettes, which I can still taste in my memory. The chickens were raised in a shed with a fenced-in yard. The fence kept the chickens in and the coyotes out – most of the time.

Milk cows were important because they provided milk, cream, skimmed milk, butter and even ice cream. (You have to keep the cow really cold when you want her to produce ice cream.) Both Tom and I learned to milk cows at an early age.

We also raised sheep for wool and meat. Mom bought "bummer lambs" from the Terwilligers, who ran a sheep ranch near Table Rock. A bum-

TOM (L) AND CHUCK (R) WITH A BUMMER LAMB ANXIOUS TO BE FED.

CHUCK AND DUCKS. COYOTES AND OTHER PREDATORS GOT MOST OF OUR UNCAGED DUCKS AND RABBITS.

mer lamb was one whose mother had died or had more lambs than she could rear. Sheep farmers sell bummer lambs at a good price. We bottle-fed the bummer lambs cow's milk, a chore I particularly liked. Mom put warm milk in a 7-Up bottle and placed a nipple on it. Tom and I fed the lambs, and they drank with the greatest exuberance, butting the bottle with their heads while wiggling their tails. We had to hold the bottle tightly so the lamb wouldn't butt it out of our hands. The lambs enjoyed the feeding so much that I couldn't help but enjoy the experience too. To this day I remember the feel and color of warm milk in a green 7-Up bottle and holding the bottle while a lamb chased after me or drank eagerly.

My parents raised goats for a while after my brother David was born because he couldn't tolerate cow's milk, which gave him colic. He did fine on goat milk but as soon as he could tolerate cow milk the goats were history. Dad didn't like goats.

We raised pigs off and on for many years. Since we had two milk cows, we had lots of skimmed milk to feed the pigs. Pigs will eat just about anything, so they got table and garden scraps also. One year I raised two pigs for a 4-H project. I named them Chop and Suey, and the best part of raising them was selling them at the Siskiyou County Fair. I found it hard to spend any quality time with pigs. They were all chore and no fun, so I was glad to get rid of them.

When we raised turkeys, we generally let them run loose around the yard. They seemed to love the grasshoppers and other bugs they could find to supplement their regular feed. They stayed close to the Red House and usually roosted in the trees just out of reach of the coyotes. Come Thanksgiving it was a bit of a chore to catch a "free range" turkey during the day, but we could usually pick one out of a tree after they retired for the night.

Of course we always had a dog or two, and plenty of cats around the place. The dogs were in charge of ranch security, but they also served as animated doorbells because their barking alerted us to real and imaginary visitors. The cats were a combination of pet and pest control. They were expected to minimize the mouse population around the house and barn.

THE BACK PORCH

A back porch is an important place on a ranch house. The Red House had a screened-in porch that ran along the east side of the house. During the summer we filled much of the back porch with wood for the winter. When the power went out, we also used wood fires in the stove or fireplace for cooking. We usually had an additional supply of wood stacked up outside, but we moved it into the back porch as soon as there was room. The back porch kept the wood dry and ready to burn when we needed it. Lugging and stacking wood was not one of my favorite chores because I always managed to fill my hands with splinters in the process.

The back porch also had a workbench and a supply of tools. Dad eventually converted half of the chicken house into his workshop, so Tom and I got to use the porch workbench for our projects. Keeping us occupied for hours, these projects consisted mostly of sawing big pieces of wood into smaller pieces and nailing them together to make what we declared to be an airplane or a gun.

Sometimes on his way home from work, Dad stopped by Eddy's Cabinet Shop in Yreka to pick up a supply of scrap wood. This was our raw material for more guns and airplanes. Of course we regularly cut and smashed our fingers, but it was all part of the learning process. The main thing I learned was that I would never be a carpenter.

For many years a hand-cranked cream separator was kept in the back porch. After Dad milked the cows in the barn, he poured some of the milk into the separator, and Tom or I would turn the handle to separate the cream from the milk. The crank was difficult to turn, and it took what seemed like an awfully long time. Dad usually finished the job when we ran out of steam.

We used a pantry in the back porch to store extra food supplies, anything that wouldn't be damaged by freezing during the winter or spoiled by the summer heat.

LIVING IN THE RED HOUSE

Our years in the rickety, ramshackle Red House created some of my favorite memories of the ranch. They were sometimes difficult but not bad times. The cold, the heat, the

THE RED HOUSE AS IT LOOKED IN THE SPRING OF 1972.

dirt, the mud, the snow, the wind, the critters – all were much more than any kid could ask for. I loved it. My folks got blisters, splinters and frostbite, while we kids had an adventure that I wouldn't trade for anything.

Along with the joys nature provided, we got a cultural education on the ranch. My father played the piano, and we were frequently treated to piano music when we lived in the Red House. Often, after putting us kids to bed, he played the piano late into the night. I remember lying in bed, waiting for sleep to come while listening to the music drifting into the back bedroom. Today, when I hear a piano playing "Rhapsody in Blue," "Deep Purple," "Prelude in C Sharp Minor" or "Hall of the Mountain King," I remember those early ranch nights and the music that filled the Red House.

IT'S NOT MUCH TO LOOK AT, PERHAPS, BUT THE RED HOUSE WAS STILL COMFORTABLE IN 1988.

The little knoll behind the house was extremely rocky, which my mother saw as a potential rock garden. Soon after we moved onto the place she had flowers growing where tumbleweeds and sagebrush couldn't. Mom always saw to it that we had a vegetable and flower garden. Even today I think of hollyhocks and morning glories when I think of Mom and the ranch. Mom could coax flowers out of the rockiest soil; she made the high desert bloom. Tom and I hauled many a gunnysack of manure from the barn so Mom could prepare the soil for her gardens. Thanks to her, we always had color around the ranch house, at least during the spring and summer months. During the winter everything turned brown or gray.

In the early years on the ranch, the electrical power was not that reliable. Today people make a big deal of it when the power goes off for a few hours. But in the late '40s and '50s, the power sometimes went out for days at a time. Mom had to cook over the wood stove or fireplace. We had candles and kerosene lanterns for light. Life went on. Nobody had telephones or battery-operated radios in the country. We knew the power company would fix the problem when they could get to it. Television was still 10 years away for us, so losing the power didn't cut into our entertainment that much.

When there was no electric power, Mom would read "Tom Sawyer" or "Huckleberry Finn" to us by candlelight. She propped up a couple of mirrors behind some candles to amplify the light and read to us until it was time to go to bed. We kids didn't miss electricity, but I'm sure Mom did. It made many things, especially cooking, more difficult for her. Fortunately, with gardens and milk cows, we were largely self-contained. If it was winter, not having a refrigerator was no problem anyway.

Not too long after we moved into the Red House, my mother got a washing machine, which she called by its brand name, the "Bendix." It was a round tub with an open top and rollers to squeeze water out of the wet clothes. The washer was stuffed into a crowded corner of the bathroom. We never had a clothes dryer while living in the Red House.

Freshly washed clothes were hung to dry inside the house on a wooden rack during the winter and outside on a clothesline during the summer. During the warm months, it seems that clothes could always be seen waving from the clothesline like colored flags in the breeze. Sometimes I would help my mother bring the clothes into the house after they were dry. She piled my arms high with fresh-smelling laundry, cautioning me not to let anything touch the ground. There's nothing that smells and feels as good as sun-dried clothes.

Many memories are tied to the Red House on the ranch. At its best it was not much more than a shack, but it was the center of a lot of rich living. We moved into the Red House at a point in my life when I was just beginning to size up the world, so it imprinted me with experiences and memories I will carry forever. It served us all well for several years until my folks built a new house up the road a bit. For many years after the excitement of the new house wore off, I longed to return to the Red House. All of the fun places to play were down there.

THE RED HOUSE IN 2004 – A FADING
REPOSITORY OF MEMORIES.

CHAPTER THREE

WHERE DOES MILK COME FROM?

Where does milk come from? People living in the city have a different understanding of this subject than people living in the country. Ask a city kid, and he or she will probably tell you milk comes from the store in a wax-coated carton or plastic bottle, and it arrives cold.

But my brothers and I were privy to inside information and learned at a tender age that milk doesn't come cold in cartons or bottles, it comes warm and it comes in cows. Some of the more sophisticated city folks know this, but they still don't have the big picture. This is the true story of where milk comes from, and I offer it for the enlightenment of all kids who had the misfortune of growing up in a city.

It is surely true that milk comes from a cow. However, not all milk comes from cows; only cow's milk comes from cows. Goat's milk comes from a goat, and I guess you can figure out where camel's milk comes from. Man obtains milk for his own nourishment from a variety of milk-producing creatures. For purposes of simplicity, we will limit our discussion to cow's milk because it's the most common and popular type of milk in our country, and it is the area of my personal experience and expertise.

If you have ever read "Grandpa's Farm," a modern children's storybook, you were probably given the impression that Grandpa and the cow have this great relationship and that the grateful cow gives Grandpa the milk because Grandpa takes such good care of the cow. This is a beautiful image and it brings tears (of laughter) to my eyes when I think about it, because it's not the *real* story. There is more to it, and perhaps it's time you learned the rest of the story.

It hurts me to be the one to tell you this, but the raw truth is that cows don't give ranchers their milk out of mutual respect and gratitude. In fact, the cow doesn't *give* the rancher milk at all; the rancher has to *wrench* it out of the cow. It's called *milking the cow,* and my brother Tom and I had to do this twice a day for many years. At some point in the process it became clear to me that this was not a work of mutual admiration; it was just work. Actually it was a chore. Ranch kids don't do work, they do *chores*, which are a lot like work. Today I don't think too many city kids hear someone say, "You kids got your chores done yet?" Or, "No TV until you do your chores and finish your homework."

At this point some city kids are wondering, "OK, if the cow doesn't give its milk to please the rancher, why do cows have milk at all?" The answer is simple. Cows produce milk for their own babies. A cow's baby is called a *calf,* and cows have milk so they can feed their babies. The cow's milk is not intended for the rancher at all; it's intended for its calf. When the rancher (usually the rancher's kid) milks the cow, he's taking the baby's milk away from it. This revelation may make some of you city kids think twice before you pour milk on your corn flakes, but it's time you learned. Life is not always what it seems.

If you have been connecting the dots, you have probably figured out that if the cow doesn't get pregnant every year, there will not be a reliable supply of milk for the rancher. In other words, no baby, no milk. This being the case, it is obviously a high priority for the rancher to make sure that the cow gets pregnant every year. How does the rancher accomplish this? Don't get ahead of me on this; it's not actually the rancher who gets the cow pregnant. It's the bull that gets the cow pregnant. No, it doesn't take place in the back seat of a tractor. The rancher introduces the cow to the bull and at the strategic time, provides a few flowers and violin music, and lets nature run its course. If all goes well, the cow eats the flowers and gets pregnant.

I hate to disillusion you further, but it is not always necessary to have a bull present for the cow to become pregnant. A process called artificial insemination can be used when the bull is out of town or out of commission. The process of artificial insemination involves a veterinarian with a shoulder-length rubber glove and a well secured cow. I watched this process a few times as a kid and decided at an early age that I didn't want to be a veterinarian when I grew up. It was bad enough watching him inseminate the cow, but I couldn't even imagine how he got the bull to cooperate in the donation end of the process. There are some things you just don't *need* to know.

If you are still tracking with me, we are at the point where the cow is kept continually pregnant so she will produce milk for her babies, so the rancher can take the milk, so he can sell it to a big business that will jack up the price and sell it to a city kid, who will pour it over his corn flakes while wondering if a baby cow is starving to death somewhere. Not to worry. The calf is not starving, but you're not going to like what I have to tell you next.

When the blessed event finally arrives and the calf is born, the rancher may magnanimously allow the calf to stay with the mother for a few days. During this time, the calf has all the milk it can handle. This situation is fine with the cow and calf, but it's not doing the rancher all that much good. The rancher has to separate the calf from the cow so he gets some of the milk too.

Here's how we accomplished it on the Nelson Ranch. The cow is brought into the barn and locked into the stanchion (a wooden device that holds its head in place) in the normal fashion for milking. The calf is taken away and locked into an adjoining pen in the barn. We don't tell either of them at the time, but they will never see each other again until the calf is well weaned. The cow is milked in the normal way, but a sizeable portion of the milk is poured into a separate bucket for the calf.

Calves know without any training how to get milk from their mother by sucking on a teat, but they don't have a clue about drinking milk from a bucket. How do you teach a calf to drink milk from a bucket? It's fairly easy. With the bucket of milk in hand, you straddle the calf and back it into the corner of the pen. You place the bucket in front of the calf, put your hand over the top of the calf's nose and slip a finger into the calf's mouth. The calf instinctively begins to suck on your finger. While the calf is sucking your finger, you lower its nose into the bucket of milk. Now, while sucking your finger, the calf is also sucking in milk. At this time you can slip your finger from the calf's mouth, and the calf continues to suck the milk from the bucket. After a few such sessions, the calf has it figured out and is ready and eager to drink the milk from the bucket all by itself.

As the calf grows older and can eat solid foods, you can give it less and less milk, and more hay and grain. Eventually the calf eats only hay and grain and is fully weaned from milk, so the rancher gets it all. When the calf is old enough, it's released into the pasture to graze with its mother and the other cattle...but not to live happily ever after.

At the appointed time, the calf is brought back into the barn, where the rancher gives it bountiful amounts of grain and hay for several weeks. The result of this special treatment is called marbling, and it makes the difference between range-fed, choice and prime beef. Ranch kids learn not to name, make pets of or otherwise become bonded to livestock, because they are food. City kids don't name the steaks on their plates, and ranch kids don't name their steaks on the hoof.

So, let's review. Where does milk come from? It comes from cows that get pregnant and produce milk for their babies, but the rancher takes the milk from the baby and keeps it for himself. He then eats the cow's baby and seduces the cow to become pregnant again so the cycle will continue. The rancher, the cow and the bull are all locked together in a rhythm of birth, milk, beef and death. In a good year, they all make out well. In a bad year, the bull still does OK.

Knowing all of this will not necessarily make your next glass of milk taste better, but at least you know the truth. For the squeamish, there's always tofu and soy milk; but, as my father would say, "It won't put hair on your chest."

CHAPTER FOUR

THE ART OF "FROGGING"

Late spring and early summer brought hot days to the ranch. During this season a special event took place at the end of each day. After the sun had settled behind the hills and the light dimmed to a reddish-orange glow in the western sky, a sound arose from the irrigation ditch that ran near the Red House. A chorus of frogs celebrated the arrival of the coolness of evening after the heat of the day.

The chorus always began with solo performances, first one, then another, then another. Before you knew it the air was filled with the voices of happy frogs. I called them *ricketeers* because that's how they sounded to me. Each frog with its own voice, some high, some low, some near, some far, inserted themselves to the chorus one by one until they reached a joyous crescendo echoing up and down the ditch as far as you could hear.

First you would hear a nearby frog give a shrill call, "*ricket, ricket,*" then one with a deeper voice and farther away would answer, "**rocket, rocket.**" Then another mid-range voice would enter in, "racket, racket." Gradually other vocalists, near and far, would join the chorus; and it would sound like,

"*Ricket, ricket,* **rocket**, racket, *ricket,* **rocket**, racket, racket, *ricket, ricket,* **rocket**, racket, *ricket,* racket."

I loved the ricketeers' concerts, and they drew me like a magnet to the banks of the irrigation ditch. The frogs' joyful chorus probably had a lot more to do with mating frenzies than celebrating dusk, but it was a happy sound and marked the arrival of the evening hours and relief from the day's hot sun.

The problem with frogs is that they don't like to sing in public. Once I lifted my head over the edge of the irrigation ditch to where I could see and be seen by the frogs, the chorus stopped instantly. Like turning off a light switch, it went from a raucous chorus to absolute silence in an instant. "Dang!" I ducked down and snuck along the bank of the ditch to a new place and slowly lifted my head over the edge until I could see the water in the ditch. Then I lay very still with my chin in my hands and waited. The cool evening breeze flipped my hair and filled my nose with the smells of wet grass, mud and ditch water. Mosquitoes bit me, but I'd have to endure them because I couldn't move. After a few minutes one frog would start, then another. Soon the whole ditch would be ringing with ricketeers. In the dimming light I could see movement as each frog's throat expanded with each *ricket*, **rocket** or racket.

When you are a kid, you can appreciate the frogs' serenade and enjoy watching them for a while, but it is soon time for something more. That something more is what is called *frogging*, an art form that every self-respecting ranch kid develops at an early age.

I got pretty good at frogging, if I do say so myself, so to make sure the sport continues into future generations, I will share some of the secrets of my success. Frogging doesn't take skill so much as it requires patience and a willingness to get wet and muddy. This is real important because it is definitely part of the process, and sopping clothes and filthy hands and feet can be displayed with pride as long as they're accompanied by a captured frog.

There are two general categories of frogging. One is ditch frogging and the other is river frogging. Ditch frogging, as the name implies, is when you catch frogs in an irrigation ditch. River frogging may sound like only a slight variation, but it is entirely different and involves stalking bullfrogs in the river. Each type of frogging requires a different skill set, so I will describe them separately.

DITCH FROGGING

Ditch frogging begins with recognizing the sound of frogs. The ranch reverberates with lots of sounds from crickets, birds, squirrels, mosquitoes and frogs. If you can't tell the difference, you might end up frogging in a rock pile or a tree where you won't have much luck. If you can distinguish a frog sound, you can follow it to its source, which in my considerable experience is going to be an irrigation ditch. Once you have this figured out, you can just stake out the irrigation ditch and wait for the sun to set. Frogs don't usually sing until the sun goes down.

Once the sun sets and you can hear the frogs going at it, you have to sneak up on the irrigation ditch. It's necessary to approach on your hands and knees from below, on the green pasture side of the ditch. If you try to creep up on the dry or uphill side, you will make a lot of noise in the dry grass and get foxtails in your socks. The green pasture side is softer and quieter, but there are some hazards to avoid there also.

Chief among these perils are cowpies and thistles. It's hard to distinguish them in post-sunset lighting, so the best thing is to avoid putting your hand or knees on anything that is darker than the surrounding area. It's fairly easy to recognize that you have touched a cowpie or thistle after the fact, but it's best just to avoid them in the first place. There is always the possibility of putting your hand or knee on a snake while creeping through the grass, but it would probably be a gopher snake or a water snake, rather than a rattlesnake. Gopher snakes and water snakes go frogging too. If it happens to be a rattlesnake, I highly recommend not messing with it. Rattlesnakes are notorious for not taking teasing well.

As you approach the ditch, you should head for the loudest frog because it's either the closest or the biggest. When frogging, ranch kids unanimously agree that it's neater to catch a big one than a small one. You have to be real quiet as you reach the edge of the ditch because the slightest noise will stop the frogs from singing. You also have to lift your head up over the ditch bank really, really slowly so they won't see the movement. If they see or hear you and stop singing, you might as well back away and start over in another place because you won't see your target frog in the dim light until you can hone in on the sound and see the movement of the frog's throat when it's singing.

Once you have identified the closest frog, fix your eyes on it and don't look away. Ideally it will be on your side of the ditch because that generally means less soaking and mud for you. Start moving ever so slowly toward your target frog, and forget all the others. Regardless of how slow and quiet you are, at some point as you move toward it, you will be seen; and all the frogs, including your target frog, will clam up. That's OK because you have locked on to your target frog. You know exactly where it is.

For some reason, your typical frog won't jump into the water and swim away even though it sees you. As long as you continue to move very slowly and quietly, it will just sit there thinking it is well camouflaged, probably because it *is* almost invisible and it's working with a frog brain. The objective is to get within an arm's length of the target frog. This is known as your *grab range*. It's necessary for you to have an accurate estimation of the length of your arm, and it may require that you extend yourself over the ditch bank as far as you can without losing your balance.

The critical time in ditch frogging is when you have achieved grab range with respect to your target frog. Frogs seem to know when you are within grab range, and many a frog has taken a preemptive hop and escaped before I could make my move. When you make the transition from stalking to grabbing, it must be a fully committed, rapid, single movement. Remember to keep *visual lock* on your target frog, and don't try to grab just the frog. Grab for the entire area that surrounds the frog. In a successful grab you will usually come up with a frog and a handful of mud and moss. All you have to do then is separate the mud and moss from the frog, and you have your prize. In all probability, both hands and at least one knee will have ended up in the ditch, but that's what it takes to become an expert ditch frogger. If the frog was on the far side of the ditch, the collateral soiling of your person and clothing will be greater than it would be if the frog were on the near side of the ditch.

Once you have captured your target frog, keep a tight grip on it and move away from the ditch. Too many times I have had a frog slip between my fingers and jump back into the ditch. The first thing you have to do with a captured frog is to show it to someone. You have expended considerable time and energy to capture this wild animal, and you deserve recognition for the risks taken and skills exercised. It has been my observation that mothers tend to be more impressed with frogging skills than fathers or brothers.

I have found that frogs are intellectually rather dim and hard to train as pets. I wish I could list 101 uses for a captured frog, but I can't. After playing with them for a while, I usually let them go in the horse-watering trough or shoved them into my pocket to save for another day. Frogs dry out rather fast in your pocket, so don't expect much entertainment value from your trophy frog after a day or so in there. Although Mom applauded my frogging exploits, she mentioned more than once that she did not enjoy the removal of dehydrated frogs – along with string, rocks and toys – when she emptied my pockets to wash my muddy clothes.

RIVER FROGGING

River frogging is quite different from ditch frogging. River frogs are larger, mostly bullfrogs rather than the little hoppers you find in irrigation ditches. Bullfrogs are not *ricketeers*. Like the ditch frogs, bullfrogs sing mostly in

A PRIME SPOT FOR BULLFROG GIGGING ON THE SHASTA RIVER.

the evening or at night, but you might hear one anytime. They don't sing nearly as much as ditch frogs, but when they do it's a deep **raaauuummm, raaauuummm, raaauuummm**. Their call faintly resembles the bellow of a distant bull, and I suspect that's how they got their name. The call of a far-off bullfrog is one of the familiar sounds I associate with a hike along the river.

Bullfrog legs are edible, but you have to get a lot of them to make a meal. We only ate them a time or two. As I recall they tasted something like chicken. In any event frog legs are easier to swallow if you think of them as chicken instead of frogs. Even though frog legs could be classified as "fast food," I don't expect to see Kentucky Fried Frog Leg restaurants any time soon.

I didn't do much river frogging in the early years on the ranch because I was too young to go the mile down to the river by myself. Most of my river frogging experience occurred during my early teens.

We kids weren't the only frog hunters along the river. Snakes were out there right along with us, but they didn't seem to mind getting muddy or wet. On more than one occasion I watched a snake eat a frog. They don't settle for the legs, they eat the whole frog. Usually we heard the frog first. He would be making an unhappy croaking sound that drew us close. When we located the source of the lament, we would find a large water or gopher snake with a frog in its mouth. In case you're not aware, snakes don't chew their food, they swallow it whole. When I was a kid I sometimes ate like a snake, but my folks wouldn't let me do it at the dinner table.

Anyway, when we arrived at the source of the sorrowful croaking sound, we would find a frog, usually with one or more of its hind legs in the snake's mouth. The process takes a while, so it's best to look for some shade and sit down. Slowly the snake would unhinge its jaw and leisurely, bit by bit, swallow the frog. Through the whole process the frog complained. It didn't look like it was very much fun for the frog or the snake. Finally the frog was silent. It was just a big lump in the snake's long, slender body. The snake then yawned and twisted its head as it reattached its jaws.

After watching the process I decided that I was glad that people don't eat like snakes. How would you like to celebrate Thanksgiving by swallowing a whole turkey and then sit there looking like you just ingested a bowling ball? Everybody would have to have his or her own turkey too. I guess you'd have to put the cranberry sauce inside the turkey before you choked it down.

Catching a river frog is more difficult than catching a ditch frog. Like ditch frogs, they are skittish, and it's not easy to get close to them. You almost never get within grab range. When they hear you coming along the riverbank or see your movement, they make a noise like *geeep* and jump with a splash into the deep water and swim away. When you're hiking along the river, you keep hearing *geeep* – splash, geeep – splash, and you know that you've just spooked some more frogs. You generally have to be walking very slowly and looking for them to see a river frog before it *geeep* – splashes on you.

There are two ways that I know of to catch a river frog; you can *fish* for them or you can *gig* them. I was never particularly good at either technique, but I did get the occasional frog.

You don't normally set out to fish for frogs. You fish for frogs when you're fishing for fish and come across a frog that doesn't *geeep* – splash. If the frog just sits there, you can easily switch from fish fishing to frog fishing.

To be a successful frog fisher, you have to be real quiet and slow in your movements. First you need to select a good lure. One with some hair or feathers on it seems to work best. Once the lure is on the line, use the fishing pole to reach out over the riverbank so you can keep a low profile and a good distance from the frog. Slowly lower the lure down in front of the frog and bounce it a bit to make it look like a bug flying around. When the frog gets tired of looking at the lure, it will sometimes zip its tongue out and snatch the lure into its mouth. When this happens, you give the line a tug to set the hook and reel him in. It's as simple as that.

When you have successfully landed the frog, detach it from the hook, put the frog into your creel and keep on fishing. At

SHASTA RIVER AT SUNSET – WHEN THE FROGS COME OUT.

the end of your expedition you can present the frog along with the fish to your mother for appropriate disposition. If you don't catch any fish, it's important to remember that you caught a frog because if you put your creel away without removing the frog, you set yourself up for a surprise the next time you go fishing. It can give you quite a stir when you put your hand into what you think is an empty creel and feel something moving. So far as I know, a bullfrog can live at least three weeks in a dry creel hanging on a nail on the back porch. At the end of three weeks they look something like living green jerky – but just barely living.

The other way to snag a frog is to gig them. A frog gig looks like a small pitchfork with barbs. The gig is attached to the end of a long pole, and you are supposed to spear the frog with it.

A proper frog gigging expedition is done from a boat with a flashlight at night. We tried this a few times and decided it was too much of a hassle to lug a boat to the river, find a good gigging spot and fight off the mosquitoes long enough to get a mess of frogs. We probably gigged ourselves as often as we gigged any frogs. Frog gigging isn't as much fun as fishing for frogs. It's difficult to balance in a boat while managing a paddle, a flashlight and a frog gig, all the while swatting mosquitoes that are ever so glad to find you in *their* swamp. Did you know that when you drop your flashlight into the river at night you can see exactly where it is by the glowing – even if you can't reach it?

CHAPTER FIVE

TAKING A HIKE

As a kid on a large ranch with many places to go and things to do, hiking was my chief source of entertainment as well as mobility. While ranch kids learn to drive at an early age, before we were allowed behind a steering wheel we walked everywhere we went. Even after I could drive, there were places I wanted to go that roads and cars couldn't take me, so walking or hiking continued to be a large part of my life. Hiking was more than a means of getting from one place to another; it was an experience in itself.

Hiking is the process by which you go *up*, *down* or *over* to someplace. You hike *down* to the lake or *down* to the river, or you may hike *over* to visit the neighbors or *up* to Eagle Peak. When we had visitors we invariably hiked down, up or over somewhere. If there was fresh snow on the ground, it was an occasion for a hike. If we wanted to go swimming on a hot summer day, we often hiked the mile down to the river and back.

I'm not sure what the difference is between a walk and a hike, but I think it has something to do with distance and conditions. A hike is usually to get somewhere, and a walk isn't necessarily going anywhere intentionally. When city people go for a walk, they usually aren't going any place in particular and the conditions are usually pretty good. They walk on paths or sidewalks, or at worst through a vacant lot. On the ranch, a hike involved climbing over rocks, dodging snakes, getting foxtails in your socks, throwing rocks at blue-belly lizards and getting bitten by mosquitoes. As I would define it, a hike is longer, hotter or colder, and more interesting than a walk. A walk is for no particular reason, but a hike is to get down, up or over to someplace in order to do something.

HIKING DURING THE "STONE AGE"

One of the primary reasons to go for a hike would be hunting. Nobody has to tell a country boy to go hunting. It's just something he does...because it's there. Hunting starts at an early age when you begin throwing stones to see if you can hit something. At some point you decide that you are going to be the best darned rock thrower there ever was. Everywhere you go, you are throwing rocks. Early on you learn that the house, the livestock and brothers are not appropriate targets, but just about everything else is. First, you try to hit another rock, a tree or a fencepost, then to see if you can hit a grasshopper on a sagebrush or a lizard on a rock, or you think, "Bet I can hit that bird." When I went for a hike I loaded my pockets with good throwing rocks and kept my eyes open. I feared no coyote because I was confident I could kill it with a single rock. The same went for mountain lions, dragons or any other predator I might encounter on a hike.

In reality, the birds and animals were quite safe during the Stone Age. So were most of the other rocks, trees and fence post targets for that matter. I never got really accurate, although I continued to harbor visions of becoming a famous rock thrower someday.

THE "SLINGSHOT AGE"

L/R: DAVE, CHUCK, TOM. DAVE IS HOLDING A SLINGSHOT MADE BY HIS OLDER BROTHERS DURING THE "SLINGSHOT AGE."

The first step up from rock throwing was a slingshot. We learned about slingshots from the Maxey brothers, Dudley and Boyd. They lived about a mile and a half east of the Red House, as the magpie flies. We met the Maxeys at school, and when we learned that we were neighbors we started hiking together.

Dudley and Boyd were slingshot sharpshooters. We had never seen such high-tech weaponry before, so Tom and I were impressed, both with the technology and their prowess with it. Whenever Dudley and Boyd came to visit, they always had slingshots hanging out of their back pockets.

We would set out in whatever direction seemed interesting at the moment. When a bird was spotted within slingshot range, Dudley or Boyd pulled out his weapon, loaded it with an appropriate rock and *SNAP......whizzzzzz.......BLAP,* down went the bird in a cloud of feathers.

This was impressive: the skill, the hunt, the technology, the kill. We were actually hunting. There are not a lot of uses for a dead bird, but the Maxey brothers showed us one thing you could do with it. The Maxeys often carried a tin can and a potato with them. When a particularly fine bird was killed while we were hiking far from the house, we prepared a meal. First we'd cut up the potato with a pocketknife and put it in the tin can. We would start a fire and put the potato-can in the middle of it. If we remembered to bring some salt and pepper, wrapped in wax paper, we sprinkled it on the potato. While the potato was cooking, we plucked the bird's feathers and gutted it. We cut a green branch from a tree for a spit, ran it through the carcass and roasted our prey while the potato continued to cook. Soon we had a "delicious" bird and potato lunch.

I could tell you it tasted like chicken and was really mouth-watering but, in truth, it tasted a lot like dead blackbird and burned potatoes. We always singed our fingers on the hot tin can and our mouths on the potatoes. A little blackbird goes a long way, but we always agreed that it was really good. "This is the life," we'd say. We were living off the land like real pioneers.

Many years later while hiking on the ranch as an adult, I shot a bird and roasted it for "old times' sake." It was hor-rible. The meat stretched farther than the rubber on our slingshots, and it tasted a lot like rubber too. It could be an acquired taste, but I think I'd rather acquire a taste for starvation than try that again.

The introduction of slingshots was a significant event at the ranch, and it brought Tom and me from the Stone Age to the age of advanced weaponry. We carefully studied the Maxey brothers' slingshots, and they shared their technol-ogy freely. Fashioning a slingshot starts with finding a good Y-shaped branch in a tree. You have to climb a lot of trees and inspect a lot of branches before you find just the right "Y" for a proper slingshot.

When we finally managed to find just the right "Y," we had to sneak Dad's saw out of the shop to cut it out of the tree. Removing your future slingshot from a tree requires the ability to balance on a limb while sawing another limb that's usually just out of reach. The best branches always seem to be just beyond your grasp. The sawing is tough because the limb you are trying to cut starts wiggling back and forth as you saw through it. Meanwhile, the limb you are balancing on also starts to wiggle to the rhythm of your sawing. With the limb you are holding on to wiggling back and forth and the one you're standing on wiggling up and down, you can find yourself going in too many directions at once. In the process we usually fell out of the tree a couple of times and got a lot of pitch and a cut or two on our hands. These were minor inconveniences and technical difficulties that we considered part of the price of a good slingshot.

With an appropriate "Y" cut from a tree, the next objective was to attach a rubber strap to the tips of the "Y." Today, it may be difficult to find rubber for such a project, but in the early days on the ranch, rubber was in plentiful supply. In the 1950s, automobile tires contained rubber inner tubes that were great for inflating and floating on the river, and for cutting into slingshot straps. It seemed there was always an old inner tube in the corner of a shed that we could use to make our slingshot straps.

It was difficult to cut a rubber strap from the tube because Mom wouldn't let us use her good scissors or kitchen knives. We resorted to whatever sharp instruments we could find or whatever discarded scissors we were allowed to use. We carried pocketknives, but they were so dull, the only thing they could cut was our fingers, which they did with regularity.

Rubber is difficult to cut with a dull instrument because it's, well, rubber. It bends and distorts instead of cutting. If you work diligently, eventually you get a hole through the tube, and from there you can saw your way around the tube to liberate the slingshot strap.

The strap is attached to the "Y" by cutting a slot in each of the upper tips of the "Y" and pulling the ends of the rubber through the slots. The ends of the strap are folded back and secured in place with as much string as you can get your hands on. When the ends of the rubber strap are properly secured to the upper tips of the "Y," you have a working slingshot.

With this new weapon in hand, I hiked the ranch in search of targets. I abandoned my goal of becoming a famous rock thrower and set my sights on becoming a renowned sling-shot shooter. Unfortunately I never achieved this goal either. Neither Tom nor I became as proficient with a slingshot as the Maxey brothers were, but we welcomed the high-pow-ered armament. I always felt safer hiking the ranch armed with a slingshot. I also found that it was easier to hit a cow with a slingshot than a bird, but this discovery had to be made when Dad was away at work.

Our friendship with the Maxey brothers was advantageous in many ways. The Maxeys were a little older, and we learned a lot from them. I don't think Mom approved of every les-son, but in addition to slingshots, they taught us how to make nifty box kites out of sticks and newspaper, dart blowguns and corncob pipes, and how to train magpies as pets.

Tom and I had our first overnight camping experience with the Maxey brothers. We camped on the riverbank near a spring at the south end of the ranch. It was cold and damp, and I nearly starved, but I was hooked on camping. It was scary camping at night, but I never felt entirely alone as long as I knew that there were 10,000 mosquitoes hovering just above my sleeping bag waiting for me to expose some skin.

THE BB GUN AGE

WITH HIS TRUSTY BB GUN IN HAND, CHUCK PROUDLY DISPLAYS HIS TROPHY (DEAD BIRD) TO HIS MOTHER, WHO DOCUMENTED THE OCCASION WITH A PHOTOGRAPH.

The next step up from the slingshot in our childhood arm's race was the BB gun. We did experiment briefly with the sling, as in David and Goliath, but found it less than satisfactory. Our slings consisted of two straps of leather with a pocket in the middle to hold a rock. We spun the sling over our head and released one of the straps when the sling reached maximum rotation. A sling could send a rock flying at high speed, but we never could figure out in advance where it would go. After a series of misfortunes and near misses with the sling, we migrated from the slingshot to the BB gun.

The Christmas morning when I opened a package to find my first Daisy BB gun is one to remember. It made me feel grown up, and I could hardly wait to go for a hike with my gun. Dad showed me how to use it, gave me a safety lecture, enumerated all off-limits targets and I was "gone hunting."

I intended to become a world-famous BB gun shooter, and I had 1,704 acres of targets to practice on. I shot rocks, bottles, tin cans, birds, frogs and bugs. Anything that wasn't specifically designated as off-limits became a valid target. Some forbidden targets were irresistible, and again I found that a cow was easier to hit than a bird.

With the advent of the BB gun came the concept of limited ammunition. As long as I was throwing rocks or shooting a slingshot, the rocky landscape provided an inexhaustible supply of ammunition. With a BB gun, I learned that it was possible to run out of ammo, and when that happened, I was dead in the water. There were so many targets and so few BBs.

Without personal assets with which to purchase BBs, it became necessary for the first time to conserve ammunition. At the same time, I more or less continuously lobbied Mom and Dad to buy more BBs. Without BBs, my Daisy gun was just dead weight. Hiking without a loaded gun was like hiking naked, only without the stickers and sunburn.

I soon learned to judge the size of my ammunition supply by tipping the barrel down and up, and listening to the pellets rolling in the magazine. I could tell when I was down to about my last 10 shots, and this was my signal to pick my targets carefully. If my remaining shots were below 10, there would be no more target practice; I would save my ammo for live game.

Birds were my favorite prey, although shooting a blue-belly lizard off a rock was a common practice. If I managed to shoot a bird, I would pick it up to check it out and carry it around for a while. If I was close to the house I would show it to Mom, and she never ceased to be amazed at my marksmanship. As I had learned during the slingshot age, there are few uses for a dead bird, so the cats usually got a treat. If I was too far from the house to bother with carrying a dead bird all the way back, I made sure there was blood on my hands so I could retain bragging rights back at the house.

On one occasion a seagull landed in the yard behind the Red House. Seagulls frequently passed through the area during the spring. It was the first time I had seen a seagull up close. I was impressed with its size and decided that it was "big game" and would make a great trophy. I poked the barrel of my BB gun out the back door of the Red House, took aim and nailed it with a shot to the head. When I saw the seagull keel over, I put the gun down and ran to collect my trophy. As soon as I picked up the biggest bird I ever shot, I realized that it wasn't dead; I had just stunned it. The seagull was alive and demonstrably irritated.

I soon found that an irritated seagull could be a flopping, scratching, pecking machine, so I was forced to let it go in fairly short order. While I tended to my scratches, the seagull flew away, apparently no worse for the wear.

HIKING WITH REAL GUNS

Eventually BB guns gave way to a .22 rifle, larger-caliber guns and more serious hunting. Dad encouraged us to shoot rockchucks and squirrels around the irrigated pastures, and Mom authorized us to shoot rabbits and squirrels around her garden. These varmints and rattlesnakes were prime targets on extended hikes. Occasionally there were more interesting targets such as coyotes and porcupines. Hunting and hiking went together, and from the time I was allowed to carry a real gun, I almost never went for a hike unarmed.

When we were older, Tom and I went hunting for deer, ducks and geese. Serious hunting was a great sport that combined the outdoors, adventure and skill. It made us proud too when Mom would serve a meal and announce that the entrée came from Tom's goose or Chuck's buck.

When I look back I remember enjoying the hunt, but I regret that I killed more critters than I needed to and certainly more than I should have. Today I think twice before I shoot at anything that isn't a hazard or a problem. I enjoy watching squirrels, rabbits and birds, and do most of my shooting with a camera. When I was a kid, almost everything that moved was a target. Today I feed the "targets" in my back yard and shoot at them with a different kind of Canon.

HIKING TO VISIT BETSY

Living on the ranch provided many advantages, but the isolation of country living was one minor downside. When school was out, we didn't see much of other kids. Kids who grow up in town can play with neighbors all the time, but in the country I only had my brothers. Sometimes we had company out to the ranch and sometimes we went visiting, but most of the time we were on our own and learned to entertain ourselves.

The ranch that adjoined our northern border belonged to Charlie Drummond. Charlie was a bigger-than-life character and scary to me as a little kid. He had a large black beard and was somehow less approachable than most other adults I knew. He lived with his wife Tassie and daughter Betsy in a house that was a little more than two miles from the Red House. Charlie was some kind of naturalist with roots on the East Coast, but that's all I knew. In the Drummond family, each family member took on a name from nature; Charlie was known as "Crow," and Tassie was "Possum." Somehow the names seemed to fit their personalities. I don't remember Betsy's

OWL'S HEAD AS SEEN FROM NEAR FAINTING SPRING.

adopted name, perhaps "Beaver," but it should have been "Horse" because she always gamboled and snorted like a wild horse.

Betsy was a few years older than I was, but she was a good friend where friends were long between and far apart. When I wanted to play with a friend, I sometimes hiked over to the Drummonds to visit Betsy. It was a long, hot hike on a summer day for a 6- or 7-year-old, but that's what you had to do if you wanted a playmate. Neither the Drummonds nor the Nelsons had a telephone in those days, so visiting was just a matter of hiking over there and hoping they were home. Of course, like most country people, they were almost invariably home. After a two-mile hike on a hot and dusty road, I would be parched, and I remember how good it was to drink the glass of cold water Possum gave me.

Possum had a unique, rather deep and syrupy voice with a raspy sound to it. She always welcomed my visits, and I liked to listen to her. Crow didn't talk to me very much, but that was fine with me because he was so intimidating. Betsy was a girl and a friend, but not a girlfriend. At the age of 6 or 7 it didn't enter my mind to pursue a girlfriend, but I did think Betsy was pretty – for a girl.

When I hiked over to visit Betsy, we invariably did what country kids do. We went for a hike. She liked to play "horse," so we would pretend we were wild horses and gallop through the junipers. Betsy had all the horse movements and noises down pat. She would toss her long black hair like a mane, stamp her feet, snort, whinny and bolt away like a spooked horse. I just galloped along feeling a bit self-conscious but glad to have the company. Sometimes we just hiked and explored different rocks, hills and lakes in the area. When we were tired of hiking we went back to the house, and I would load up on cool water and hike the two miles back home.

HIKING FOR A SWIM

The Shasta River runs along the south and west side of the ranch and offers good swimming during the hot summer days. Before we could drive, we would often hike down to the river for a swim. From the Red House, the route to the river ran mostly through irrigated pastures. Since we were often barefooted, the hike required us to dodge fresh cowpies and to make sure we didn't step on a thistle or a bee in the clover. Given a choice between a thistle, a bee and a cowpie, we would probably prefer to step on a cowplop; it's not painful and you could wipe it off on the grass in the pasture. Down near the river we sometimes encountered salt grass, which is a low-growing "stickery" grass. Walking barefoot through salt grass is all pain and no fun.

Mom believed the folk wisdom that you shouldn't go into the water for at least an hour after you last ate because you might get a stomach cramp that would double you over and cause you to drown. It seemed that everybody believed that questionable advice, so we abided by it. After Tom and I ate lunch, Mom wouldn't let us head out for the river until the appropriate time had passed. (I wonder if amphibians have to wait an hour after eating before they get *out* of the water.)

Mom also set a rule that we couldn't go swimming unless the thermometer reached 80°. On most summer days the temperature would easily pass the 80° mark, but occasionally it would fall short. When Tom and I had our minds set on swimming, we would watch impatiently as the thermometer crept ever so slowly toward the designated temperature. When it appeared the thermometer was having difficulty reaching 80°, we discovered that we could expedite the situation by holding a match under it. Unfortunately, it didn't take Mom long to figure out this strategy, as the temperature doesn't usually jump from 75° to 115° in five minutes – especially when the ambient temperature still feels like 75°.

A visit to the river also meant that you were going to be bitten by mosquitoes and stung by a deerfly or two. If you were particularly unlucky, a horsefly might also bite you. Another hazard was the stinging nettles that grew in clumps in many locations along the river. Nettles have broad light-green leaves with serrated edges. They grow in tall stocks but are often hidden by other vegetation that grows along the river. An inadvertent brush against the leaves of the nettle will give you a painful sting that lasts for hours. I also had a persistent fear of stepping on a crawdad while wading through the shallow waters in the river. I never did step on one, but I sure did walk carefully and keep my eyes peeled. All of these challenges were considered minor hazards or small inconveniences compared to the pleasures of swimming in the Shasta River.

The river water was too chilly to swim in on a cold day or before about 1 p.m. on a hot day. I was a skinny kid, so I could only tolerate the river water for a short period on most days. After I got the shivers, I would have to climb out of the river, sit on the bank and cover my legs with sun-heated sand, while Tom kept swimming and hollering at me to come back into the water. Tom was better insulated against the cool river water. He called me a sissy and a chicken, but I preferred to be a warm chicken on the bank than a brave and miserable human in the river.

Swimming usually included various forms of tag, plunging off a makeshift diving board and a mud fight or two. We also made spears out of tules and played war. If there was any dunking going on, I was usually the dunkee because I was younger and smaller than Tom. Threats to "tell Mom" had little effect when we were over a mile from the house. By the time we got back to the house, all was usually forgiven.

When we got older we usually drove in a rattletrap ranch pickup rather than walking down to the river for our swims. This minimized close encounters with cowpies, thistles, bees and salt grass. The mosquitoes, deerflies and horse-flies were always glad to see us whether we arrived afoot or in a vehicle.

HUNTING ARROWHEADS

One of my favorite hiking activities was hunting for arrow-heads. Along the river there were many areas where Indians had camped. They left behind animal bones, clam-shells, lots of obsidian chips and the occasional arrowhead. Sometimes we found large flat rocks with hollowed areas that the Indians had used for grinding food. On occasion, I even found human bones where Indians had been buried.

Hunting for arrowheads is part art and part science. From a distance, it might just look like a kid wandering in circles with his head down, but there's a lot more to it. First you have to look for a location where the presence of obsid-ian chips or clamshells tells you that Indians were active in the area. Then you look for a place where they made a campfire. This is identified by a cluster of small rocks and particularly by rocks that have been cracked in two by heat from the fire or quick cooling from being dropped into a basket full of water. Sometimes you can still find charcoal chips and rocks that had been blackened by fire. These are the areas where you pay the closest attention when you are hunting for arrowheads.

Arrowhead hunting takes time and patience, and you pick up a lot of obsidian chips before you find an arrowhead. Most of the arrowheads I found were broken and had like-

KATHY & CHUCK WITH
A PIECE OF BONE THAT
LED TO THE FIND.

ly been discarded rather than lost. Over the years and many, many hours of searching, I did find a few exceptional arrowheads, but I no longer have them. While I was away at college, my mother offered my collection to a family friend who was visiting the ranch. Apparently the friend was a collector, and Mom let him pick what he wanted from my collection. Of course he took all of my best ones and left the inferior ones behind. He did leave a rather crude flint arrowhead behind in exchange. He told my mother that it came from the Lyndon Johnson ranch in Texas, but I will never know and don't really care. My arrowhead collection was special to me because I found each one on the ranch where I grew up. Sometimes mothers don't understand what's important.

SKULL UNCOVERED. NOTE
SHOVEL DAMAGE AND
POCKET KNIFE FOR SCALE.

In 1985 when visiting the ranch with my wife, Valerie, and daughter, Kathy, we made an interesting find while looking for arrowheads. We were down on the sandy flats near Salvadori Hill, and I was using a shovel to see what I could find deeper in the sand. While digging in a location that I suspected had been an Indian campsite, I turned over a shovel of sand and noticed a piece of thin flat bone. On closer inspection it looked like my shovel had nicked off part of a human skull. In a high school art class I had been required to name and draw every major bone in the human body, so I was reasonably familiar with human bone structure.

Many years earlier while searching for arrowheads in the same area, I found what appeared to be a portion of a child's lower jawbone with a tooth in it. Based on the previous find and the piece of bone

KATHY, CHUCK AND VALERIE REMOVING SAND.

in my shovel, I suspected that there might be human remains under my feet. With this in mind, we put the shovel aside and dug with our hands until we had uncovered a skull. At this point we switched to hand trowels and brushes so we could excavate further without disturbing the remains. It took us many hours of work in the hot sun, but eventually we managed to uncover a nearly complete human skeleton. The individual appeared to have been buried in a fetal position. We were careful not to disturb the bones, but we left the skeleton uncovered until my father was able to arrange

THE SKELETON AS IT LOOKED WHEN FULLY UNCOVERED.

for an archaeologist to look at it. The archaeologist told my father that the skeleton was probably a female and estimated that she had been buried for around 500 years.

Imagine that! At about the time Columbus was sailing for the New World, a Native American lady lived, died and was buried on what would one day be the Nelson Ranch. After the archaeologist had inspected the grave, it was covered over, and my father marked the grave with a simple head-piece that said "Indian." I later threw the marker away, and today the grave is unmarked and again "invisible" in the landscape.

HIKING TO FISH

My earliest memory of fishing involved sitting on the bank of the river with a fishing line tied to the end of a stick. My mother attached a hook on the end of the line, put a worm on it and threw it in the river. Then we sat there waiting for some-thing to happen. At first it seemed rather boring, but then I could feel a gentle tug. Mom said, "Isn't there something on your line?" Sure enough, I had caught my first fish. She

CHUCK (FOREGROUND) FISHING WITH TOM AND A COUSIN IN 1948. JESS, A HIRED HAND, LOOKS ON.

helped me pull the little trout out of the river, and I carried it around on the end of my line showing it to anybody who would pay at-tention. The fish and I were both hooked on that day.

As the years went by, my interest in fishing increased. I was not particularly fond of the flavor of fish, but I enjoyed fishing. Fishing for me was not entirely about catching fish; it was an excuse for taking a hike. I liked to hike along the river, seeing and hearing the wildlife, breathing in the smells of the river and trying not to step into one of the many muskrat holes that were hidden by the tall grass along the river.

The more you fish, the more you learn how to read the river and identify the good fishing holes. In time you learn where to throw your line and how to guide your lure to the right place. I prefer to fish using lures because there is more action to it than there is with bait fishing. The *Shasta Shiner* is my favorite lure, but I can't name everything in my tackle box as "real fishermen" can. I like to cast a few times then move on to another hole. The hike is as important as the fishing. Of course there is the little stir of excitement when you feel a fish hit your lure and the thrill of catching a "big one," but fishing is mostly something to do while you are enjoying being there.

Larry Jones, a high school friend living in the Big Springs area, was one of my occasional fishing partners. I usually fished alone, but it was always nice to have a friend along. Larry liked to fish using worms and I preferred lures, so we had an ongoing debate about which was the better way to fish and which one of us was the better fisherman.

CHUCK WITH A 21-INCH TROUT IN 1992.

Larry was clearly the more accomplished fisherman (and he could probably name everything in his tackle box too), but we enjoyed our friendly debates and often had contests to see who could catch the most fish in a given time period using our respective techniques. During the competitions, we hiked our way down the river, hitting all the good holes we knew so well. The contests were not entirely fair since Larry frequently gave me first crack at the best fishing holes, a privilege that came with being the property owner's son. For the most part the contests ended in a draw. I tended to catch slightly more fish with my lures, and Larry tended to catch larger fish with his worms. In fishing you get points for both "more" and "larger," so we called it a draw and both retained bragging rights. When you're fishing everybody wins – except the fish.

When hiking along the river, whether fishing or not, there is always something going on that can be appreciated. It may be a hawk's piercing call as it circles over your head, or it may be a bullfrog croaking somewhere downriver. Sometimes your heart skips a beat as a previously unseen pheasant at your feet takes sudden flight with a loud squawk and the thunder of wings. Occasionally you will get too close to a dove or killdeer nest, and the parent bird will suddenly appear, fluttering and flopping around on the ground as if it has a broken wing. When I was young, this deception worked really well on me. I would chase after an "injured" bird only to find out that, after it had led me far away from its nest, it would miraculously heal and fly away.

A HIKE ALONG THE LAKE IN THE EVENING IS OFTEN REWARDED WITH A STUNNING SUNSET.

There were rattlesnakes on the ranch, so we learned to hike with this in mind. My eyes were always sweeping the ground in front of me. Just for safety's sake, I didn't usually put my feet or hands anywhere I couldn't visually inspect first. Even as wary as I was, I still had an occasional close encounter with a snake. When something unexpectedly moved at my feet, I was usually airborne before I knew what it was. Typically it turned out to be a mouse or friendly snake rather than a rattlesnake. I did have a few close calls, but I never did get bitten by a rattlesnake – which I like to think was lucky for the snake.

CHAPTER SIX

RANCH DOGS

It would be hard to imagine a ranch without dogs. Every "real" ranch has to have at least one dog in residence. Ranch dogs are good for company, security and rodent extermination. Some ranch dogs are working dogs and are good for herding animals or hunting. Of course, some dogs are good for nothing, and we had a few of those too.

Through the years we had a wide, and sometimes strange, assortment of dogs on the Nelson Ranch. Ranch dogs are not usually given sophisticated names. I seriously doubt that a dog named Percival would last on a ranch. The cats would probably chase him off. Our ranch dogs had rather straightforward, if not imaginative, names like *Shep,* the Shepherd; *Mack,* the McNab; and *Goldie,* the Golden Retriever. Fortunately we never had a Shih-Tzu to name. We were busy people, so we didn't waste a lot of time trying to think of fancy names for our dogs. They all came for dinner no matter what we called them. One exception to the rule was the basset hound we named *Bacchus* after the Roman god of wine. What can I say? Somehow the name and the face went together.

SHEP, THE SHEPHERD

When I remember our ranch dogs, I always think first of Shep. "Old Shep" was not just a song title to me; he was a real dog. Shep was the first dog we had as kids, and he came with us when we moved onto the ranch in 1947. Shep was some sort of a shepherd with shaggy black, brown and white hair. Every kid should grow up with a dog, and Shep and I matured together. I don't remember Shep too much when he was a puppy. In my earliest memories, I just recall him as shaggy like a mop, with a bobbed tail on one end and a tongue on the other, full of motion and full of life.

Shep was not particularly smart or clever as dogs go, but he was everything a ranch dog named Shep should be. If I was away for a while, Shep was always glad to see me, though not hysterically glad, as some high-strung dogs are. Shep always tried to be obe-

FAITHFUL SHEP PLAYS ALONG WITH CHUCK IN IMPROVISED CARDBOARD BOATS ON THE LAWN AT THE RED HOUSE.

dient, but some things are too much to ask of a dog. To be honest, Shep probably wasn't much good for anything but keeping us company, but he did that very well. Shep was a friend as well as a dog. You could always talk to Shep, and he would listen. You could tell he was paying attention by the way he looked at you and wagged his tail. He had to "speak" back to you through his eyes and his tail, and he could be pretty articulate. That's what made Shep a good dog.

Shep had some specialties, and chasing rabbits and squirrels were at the top of the list. Unlike many dogs we had on the ranch, Shep actually caught up with them once in a while. Some of our other dogs chased rabbits and squirrels as a sort of gentleman's sport. It wasn't that way with Shep. He appeared to chase them because he considered them to be encroaching on *his* territory. He chased critters because he saw it as his job or obligation. When Shep caught up with an animal, he would grab it by the neck, give it a quick, hard shake and it was all over. Once the critter was dead, Shep was done with it. Sometimes one of the other slow-running dogs would come in behind Shep, pick up the deceased prey and carry it around for all to see. Shep did the work but the follow-up dog carried the trophy as if to say, "Look what *we* did."

Shep had a few bad habits that were apparently beyond remediation. Being all dog, he couldn't pass up a good roll in a fresh cowpie or a decaying carcass of any sort. It always seemed strange to me that a creature with such a highly developed sense of smell could delight in the overpowering stench of a dead cow. The odor we found so offensive was so pleasing to the nose of Shep that he couldn't resist coating himself with it to savor throughout the day. This was accomplished by a thorough roll in the remains of a ripe, decaying cow.

After this ritual, Shep seemed highly desirous of associating himself with us, presumably to show off his "roll-on perfume." Poor Shep never could figure out our sometimes violent reaction to his presence when he was coated with *Essence of Dead Cow.* We seemed so friendly just moments before. In the absence of a dead cow, he would sometimes roll in a fresh cowpie for the same effect. If we'd had more marketing savvy, we probably could have bottled this fragrance and sold it to dog-loving city folk as *Corral #9.*

Shep's second big hang-up was porcupines. A porcupine, as everybody knows, is covered from head to tail with needle-sharp quills. Porcupines are relatively small compared to most dogs, and, while they spend most of their time up in trees, they do travel on the ground occasionally. Whenever Shep chanced upon a porcupine out for a stroll, the chase was on...and the winner always lost. I have never seen a porcupine run or even scurry when being chased by a dog. They move slowly and deliberately and, to his detriment, Shep always caught the porcupines he chased.

The encounters were always the same; loud barking followed by a *YIKE* followed by angry barking, more *YIKES* and a leisurely retreat on the part of the porcupine. Unless we caught Shep and dragged him from the scene before he seized the porcupine, our poor dog ended up with a face full of quills. Regardless of the volume or tone of voice, our commands – "Here boy!," "Come back!," "Stop!," "Sit!" or "Go home!" – went unheeded when Shep was concentrating on a porcupine. We had to physically carry him away to avoid the encounter.

The evening ritual after Shep met up with a porcupine was always the same. Shep would present his face full of quills to Dad, who would take a pair of pliers and pull out each quill, one by one. Porcupine quills have tiny barbs like a fishhook, so they didn't come out easily. With each yank of the pliers, Shep would *YIKE* and run to the far corner of the room, where he would shake his head, tremble and bleed. Dad would say, "Come here boy!," and Shep would obediently crawl on his stomach across the room to place his trembling head between Dad's knees for the next yank and *YIKE*. This pathetic cycle was repeated as many times as was necessary until all the quills were removed.

Shep was not one to learn from his mistakes, and, in spite of the painful, pitiful evenings after, Shep continued to chase porcupines until he died. It seemed that, with each encounter with a porcupine, his determination increased. He seemed to be thinking, "I know what I did wrong last time; I'll get him this time." Unable to learn from his prior experiences, it was Shep's destiny to hurt. In my law enforcement career, a lot of people reminded me of Shep.

Like all of our dogs, Shep served as something like an organic doorbell. Since we didn't have a telephone for many years, the only way we knew we were going to have company was when they showed up. The ranch dogs gave us a head's-up. Our dogs would bark and run out to meet and intimidate any visitors who came out to the ranch. As part of the official welcome, the dogs usually peed on the tires of the visitors' car. With this ceremony accomplished, the dogs would turn to look at us to see what to do next. If we welcomed the company, the dogs quieted down and acted friendly.

CHUCK, TOM & DAVID WITH SHEP AND GOLDIE.

GOLDIE, THE RETRIEVER

Goldie, the golden retriever, was another classic ranch dog. Like Shep, she was not particularly bright, but she was a "good old girl." For a retriever, Goldie was not unduly fond of water and got nervous around guns, so she never became a retriever of game in the traditional sense. However, she managed to act out her retriever instincts as best she could by dutifully lugging around the squirrels and rabbits that Shep killed.

She also had a habit of dragging the decaying carcass of any hapless road-kill she found onto the lawn or front porch for all to enjoy. Although not as obsessed as Shep was with *Eau d'Decay*, she was not beyond a good roll in a cow carcass to obtain a coating of that bouquet that dogs find so irresistible. Goldie was very gentle and sometimes even allowed one of the ranch cats to ride around on her back. That cat was another story.

Goldie may have been intellectually challenged, but she had a big heart and a good nose that helped her earn her place of honor among ranch residents. One of my favorite Goldie memories dates back to the late 1950s when she helped me track down a deer I had shot.

On a warm autumn morning I was hunting on the west side of Government Hill when I spotted a buck with a nice-sized rack looking at me from behind a rock outcropping. The deer was about 50 yards away, and all I could see was its head and part of its neck. I was toting my mother's .30-.30 rifle. It was my favorite gun, but it was going to be a tough shot. My heart pounding with excitement, I raised the rifle and fired as quickly as I could before the buck ducked out of sight.

At first I didn't know if I had hit it because it disappeared the instant I fired. I ran to where the deer had been standing. It was long gone, but I saw some blood on the ground, telling me I had hit it. Finally I spotted it. By this time it was about 150 yards away, running west across the valley between

Government Hill and Salvadori Hill. I fired a couple useless rounds as it vanished into the trees on Salvadori Hill.

CHUCK WITH BUCK GOLDIE HELPED FIND WITH HER "GOLDEN" NOSE.

I followed the blood trail as far as I could but soon lost it. While I was walking in circles, trying in vain to pick up the trail in the rocks and bronco grass, I heard the sound of a truck and looked up to see Mom coming down the road in the pickup. Goldie, an old dog by then, was along for the ride. Mom had heard the shots from the ranch house, nearly a mile away, and had come to see if I'd had any luck. I told her what happened, and we looked for the trail together. When I showed Goldie a drop of blood, she quickly figured out what we were trying to do. She took off toward the west with her nose to the ground. She seemed to know exactly where she was going, so I ran behind, trying to keep up as best I could.

Goldie led me to a secluded thicket along the river, where I found my buck. One quick shot ensured we had venison in the freezer that year. It had a nice five-point rack that still serves as a ranch souvenir and hatrack in my garage. I would never have found that buck without Goldie – "good dog."

MACK, THE McNAB

Mack, the McNab, was an interesting case study of a dog that never made it on the ranch. Mack didn't really have a chance because he wasn't playing with a full deck. I don't know if he came that way or if my three brothers and I drove him crazy. To be honest, we did play some "head games" with him, but I suspect Mack's oars didn't reach the water when we got him, and we kids just aggravated his condition. Suffice it to say that my brothers and I did nothing for that poor dog that could conceivably be construed as therapeutic.

Upon determining Mack's tentative grip on sanity and limited intellectual capacity, we experimented by intentionally sending mixed messages. We shouted, "Good dog!" in a loud, angry voice, followed by "Bad dog," in a soft, friendly voice. On one occasion we zipped Mack into a tent that we set up on the lawn. We used to sleep in the tent on hot summer nights but we zipped Mack up in it just to see what he'd do.

His reaction was immediate doggie panic. He began hurling himself against the sides of the tent in an attempt to escape confinement. We heard a loud *WHUMP,* and the tent would bulge out in one direction, then *WHUMP* and it would bulge out in another direction. *WHUMP,* bulge, *WHUMP,* bulge. How could we have been so cruel? I'm not proud of it now, but with television still a few years away, this passed for entertainment for some hardened country kids. When we finally let Mack out, it was probably more to preserve the tent than to rescue our crazy dog.

McNabs are natural herding dogs. They love to herd animals around and naturally go for the heels instead of the head, which, when you think about it, is the best way to herd

75

a critter unless you want to herd it backwards. McNabs seem to know this instinctively, while most other dogs don't.

Mack never did learn the difference between herding for the fun of it and herding for a rancher-approved objective, such as moving the cattle from Field No. 1 to Field No. 2. Freelance herding is known as "chasing the cows," and that, along with leaving a gate open, is one of the cardinal sins on a ranch. A chased cow will lose weight or perhaps break a leg, miscarry or run into a barbed wire fence. A milk cow could suffer the same fate and reduce milk production as well. An untrained dog may also bite and injure a cow, or more likely, a calf. A dog that freelance-herds a neighbor's cows gets himself shot – and rightly so. Perhaps if we could have found some way to communicate with Mack other than cussing and waving our arms in the air, we could have saved him from his propensity to freelance.

Mack had an unusual way of getting exercise. He would run around the house in ever-widening circles. We would watch him for an hour or more as he would dash around the house, each pass a little farther out, until he would disappear from view. This became another form of mild entertainment: "Hey! Somebody turn on the dog, and let's watch him run."

While Mack was basically a friendly dog, he did show some surprisingly aggressive behavior on occasion. Once he greeted a visitor to the ranch with an unprovoked bite. The visitor wasn't really hurt, but Mack's days were numbered from that day forward. We didn't get much company out to the ranch, and if they got dog-bit or suffered a Mack attack when they came to call, they would probably quit coming after a while.

Mack's end came when he encountered a porcupine and took a tail slap across the chest. The quills worked their way into his chest cavity before we could get to them, and Mack was in such a bad way that he soon faced a merciful firing squad. We took Mack out to the bone yard, a desolate corner of the ranch where we hauled large animal carcasses, mostly cows and horses, so they would decay where they wouldn't contaminate the pastures or barnyard. Surrounded by white, sun-bleached bones, perhaps an image from dog heaven, we gave Mack his last supper. Dad and Tom fired on my command. We felt the guilt was sufficiently shared that way, and Mack became history. Death is one of the realities of ranch life, and it was Mack's turn.

BACCHUS THE GREAT!

Bacchus was perhaps our most unusual dog. He was a basset hound and not really built for ranch life. With his short legs and long body, he just didn't have the clearance he needed to negotiate his way over most of the rocks and flora indigenous to the ranch. It's a wonder he wasn't emasculated by some of his cross-country romps. Bacchus wasn't built to run gracefully through the tall grass; he was built close to the ground so he could use his incredible nose. He could smell a rabbit in the next state and tell you if it was left- or right-handed.

Bacchus couldn't run fast, and he was too low-slung to see over the bronco grass, let alone the sagebrush, so he chased his rabbits by nose rather than sight. He was sheer entertainment to watch. The other dogs usually saw the rabbit first and would *YIP* and start the chase. Bacchus would follow the procession by smell. He would announce his involvement in the chase with his loud **AHROOOO...AHROOOO**. This high-volume baying was totally out of proportion to his size, and I suppose it was driven by instinct.

Since Bacchus was chasing by nose rather than sight, he would sometimes continue going straight at locations where the chase procession that preceded him had made a sharp turn. When this happened, the **AHROOOO...AHROOO** would stop as he lost the scent trail. Then Bacchus would backtrack his own trail to where he lost the scent. Upon finding the scent trail again, he would check both directions until he established the proper direction of the pursuit, whereupon he would resume his **AHROOO...AHROOOO** as he continued in not-so-hot pursuit up the trail, in the right direction but far, far behind the chase.

Bacchus was the first and only ranch dog to be given the run of the house. Most ranch dogs are "outside dogs." Bacchus was smaller than most ranch dogs, but that's not what got him special privileges. It was his eyes. Basset hound eyes are pools of pathos. A simple glance at the door, and the family members would stumble over each other let him out. The same thing would happen if he wanted to come in the house. A pathetic glance through the window, and the door would be flung open. King Bacchus would waddle in while the other dogs looked on with pained incredulity. Why should he be welcomed in when the house was off limits for them? His dinner would be immediately served as soon as he cast his "I'm hungry" glance. It made you sick to watch that dog train us. The whole family learned to sit up, roll over and speak when Bacchus so commanded.

BACCHUS LETS IT ALL HANG OUT AS HE NAPS WITH DAN.

Having the run of the house, Bacchus would sleep where he liked. One of his favorite tricks was to climb up into the chair he found most comfortable and flop on his back with his ears and legs going in every which direction. This posture would expose his decidedly male plumbing. Despite this obscene display, we never disturbed him lest we fall victim to his disapproving glance.

REBEL, THE LAB

Rebel was a black Labrador retriever. He was a classic of the breed. He loved water and would jump into water of any color, odor or temperature without hesitation. Stagnant or clean, warm or freezing, it made no difference, he loved water. When the lake was frozen over with a thin coating of ice, Reb still loved to jump into the water. He'd break the ice as he swam to retrieve whatever we threw out there for him to fetch. After several swim-to-fetch trips in the frozen lake, Reb would be shivering so hard that we could hear his teeth chattering. Usually we would have mercy on him and quit playing fetch before he was too frozen to retrieve.

Rebel was never properly trained to retrieve for hunters, but he loved fetch and would try to catch whatever we threw before it hit the ground. This, of course, led to experimentation by my brothers and me. We found that he would gladly catch a rock in his teeth or a dried cowpie. It didn't matter to him; it was all fetch, and he loved to play fetch. In retrospect it's clear that we took advantage of Reb's instincts and low I.Q. for our own entertainment. But, then again, we all had a good time, even Reb. We loved to hear the loud *CLACK* as Reb caught a rock in the air. When he died, he had all his teeth, but it wasn't our fault.

LADY, THE LAST DOG

In my father's final years on the ranch, there was one last ranch dog. Like most of our non-pedigreed mutts, Lady was more of a community project than a pure breed. She was supposedly of Australian ancestry, consisting of something called a Queensland Heeler with a bit of Dingo thrown in. My father was up in years, and Lady was even older in "dog years." Perhaps because he was living alone on the ranch, Dad became quite attached to Lady, and they were something of a team.

Dad swore that Lady knew how to make a martini. He explained it this way: Every evening at around 5 p.m., Dad would make himself a martini then he would feed the dog. Lady was mostly an outside dog, but she spent a lot of her time sitting backwards on a chair on the patio and staring into the house through the front window. Dad put extra padding on the chair so Lady would be high enough to see in the window. I guess people watch television and dogs watch peoplevision. In any event, from this position, Lady could look right into the kitchen where Dad prepared his cocktails.

DAD AND LADY DOING CHORES TOGETHER.

Each evening at around 5 o'clock, Lady positioned herself in the window and watched while my father assembled the ingredients for his martini. When Dad put ice in the glass, Lady sat tight. When Dad added vermouth to the glass, Lady sat tight. When Dad added gin, Lady sat tight. However, when Dad put an olive in the glass,

Lady took off like a shot for the back of the house. Dad knew exactly where Lady was going and met her on the back porch to feed her. I'm not sure who had trained whom, but it was an evening ritual that both man and dog enjoyed.

Dad prepared a special recipe he fed Lady every evening. First he boiled some bones and meat in a large pot. The end product was a mess of semi-cooked meat and bones in a thick, smelly broth. This gruel was stored in a semi-functional refrigerator on the back porch. At feeding time, Dad put a bit of dry dog food in a dish, added a bone and piece of meat from the "stink-pot," and topped it off with a ladle of aromatic broth. Lady apparently considered this quite a treat as she ate it eagerly – but then I've found that dogs eat everything and anything eagerly.

I watched this ritual on occasion and decided that Dad's sense of smell must have faded along with his hearing. Lady apparently loved the taste and bouquet of her meal, but then there's no accounting for a ranch dog's sense of taste and smell.

When Lady died, Dad buried her in a proper grave on the hill behind the house where a few other special ranch dogs were laid to rest. Lady's passing must have been tough for Dad, but I didn't fully appreciate how difficult it was until I found some remarks he had apparently written down as Lady was nearing death.

I found his handwritten notes in the ranch house many years after Dad died. They amounted to a eulogy and recorded a mutual bond and respect between man and dog, while reflecting an uncharacteristic level of emotion on the part of my father.

I think Dad's tribute to Lady, an old cowboy saying goodbye to an old cow dog in his own words, is a good way to close our chapter on ranch dogs:

Lady – A Cow Dog

When we work cattle in the corral, she follows the feet of each animal through the chute and into the squeeze. Then bites them on the flank to get them out of the squeeze. She lost her lower canines doing this.

In her intensity of getting the job done, she will actually quiver all over her body. She believes she is running the whole operation. There is no nonsense to her efforts.

Lady has some newer scars now. The toe on her left hind foot is missing due to being caught in a coyote trap.

Just recently we were moving cattle, and a calf ran under the hired man's horse and she went after it. The horse, in a reflex, kicked her in the right eye. Oh, how it hurt! I nearly cried. We couldn't stop for man nor beast as we had a couple of hundred calves to brand. Lady stuck with us and continued to help but laid down frequently. The vet took bone fragments from her eye, and I treated her twice a day for a month. She can now see pretty good out of it.

Lady is a scarred-up and crippled cow dog, but still has a heart of gold and goes after them—grabbing bulls by the tail and swinging on it. She feels her mission in life is working cattle.

She is older than me – dog-wise, which is plenty. She's exhausted at the end of the day. Sometimes she has to lay all the next day – such devotion to duty! She says this is her reason for being – her purpose in life.

You cannot believe her ecstasy when she sees me putting on my riding boots. She knows what each hat and boot means – rubber ones for irrigating, shoes for ho-hum and cowboy boots, her favorite. She talks in a low growl and tells me to hurry up while I get vaccines and equipment ready.

When we start riding out, in her exuberance she will circle my horse and even nip at his heels to hurry up. I don't like this because I don't want bucking anymore.

It has taken her many years to learn how to drive cattle. At first, if there was a lagger, I'd tell her to "get 'em" and damned if she wouldn't go for the head and cut it out and make it worse. She savvys better now and works easier. I swear she is a Queensland header rather than a heeler. Oh well, I have faults too.

I cannot credit her efforts enough – such devotion, such intensity to work, if only humans could learn from her. I write this with tears in my eyes.

Sometimes I get mad at her due to my short fuse, but she has already forgiven me my weakness when I try to make up.

Lady has many memories in this old man's mind: Driving to the mail box to get mail. Mowing the lawn when she kept going to the center to get away – dumb dog. Trying to be coy to the macho police dog, but with the wrong signals as she was spayed. Watching me ladle out her feed and licking her chops. Half-heartedly chasing the cat. Letting me know when anyone comes to the house. Waiting patiently for days and hiding out when I go on a trip. The hired man feeds her, but she never appears, yet the feed is gone later. Her dancing welcome when I return.

Mankind could learn many lessons from such a faithful friend. I feel inadequate in expressing my emotions. Wherever dog heaven is, I am sure she will go there. It would be a privilege to accompany her, but I'll bet they wouldn't let me in.

Other dogs lived on the ranch, but Shep, Goldie, Mack, Bacchus, Rebel and Lady left the deepest impressions on me. Dogs are just about a necessity on a ranch. They are the first ranch representatives to greet you when you drive onto the property, and when you leave they will be the last thing you see through the dust in your rear view mirror. Proper ranch dogs bark a greeting and see you off with the same ceremony. They keep the small critters out of the garden, provide companionship and eat the leftovers you don't want to see again. They have their specialties and their eccentricities, and they are always good entertainment.

THIS PHOTO OF LADY AND THE RED HOUSE WAS
TAKEN BY SEDG NELSON ON CHRISTMAS DAY, 1983.
A NOTE ON THE BACK OF THE PHOTO INDICATES THE
TEMPERATURE WAS 20°, AND THEY WERE JUST BACK
FROM FEEDING THE CATTLE OUT ON THE RANGE.

CHAPTER SEVEN

CHICKENS FROM HATCHET TO SKILLET

Life on the ranch had its hardships, but the food was generally good unless Mom was experimenting with something. With a husband, four boys and an assortment of dogs and cats to sustain, Mom set a high priority on keeping everybody well fed, and it was undoubtedly a logistical challenge. In keeping with this priority, the ranch usually had a chicken house and a flock of chickens. With beef, pork and lamb on the hoof, and chicken on the wing, we had plenty of meat. The chickens also kept us supplied with eggs. We also had milk, cream, butter and cheese from the cows, vegetables from the garden and the occasional wild game or fish from the river. We were never in serious danger of starving to death.

To be honest, I have never had a particularly high regard for chickens. This opinion does not necessarily extend to fried chicken, but it certainly applied to the chickens we raised on the ranch. If you want to know anything at all about chickens, you could probably find it in the dictionary under "dumb." If chickens were people, you could say that they are the *personification* of dumb. Perhaps it would be more correct to say they are the *chickification* of dumb.

In any event, they are too stupid and void of personality to make good pets. Chickens don't appear to be much more than a set of basic instincts wrapped in meat and covered with feathers. If there were a market for "stupid," our chickens would have made us rich.

COLLECTING EGGS

Chickens are good for food, but they also produce other important byproducts. Eggs are one of them. Feathers are another chicken byproduct, but they taste terrible so they are usually used to stuff mattresses and pillows.

The true story about where eggs come from is even worse than the story about where milk comes from, so we won't discuss it in any detail. I had a friend who said he would never eat cow tongue because he didn't want to eat anything that came out of a cow's mouth. This seemed like a reasonable position to take, but he was somewhat inconsistent in his preferences because he liked eggs. I decided it best not to help him connect the dots; a guy like that could starve to death if he thought too much. I don't like cow tongue either, but for a different reason. I don't want to taste anything that once was capable of tasting me back.

Eggs are a natural chicken-derived product and one of the staples of ranch life. Go to any grocery store and you will usually find something called "Ranch Eggs." I seriously doubt that the chickens that laid the eggs you buy in the store ever saw a real ranch, but most people probably think "ranch eggs" taste better than "chicken-factory eggs" so that's what they call them.

The ranch eggs you buy in the store are different from the ones we had on the ranch. For one thing, our ranch eggs had deep orange yolks, while the ones you get in the store tend more toward yellow. I was told that a chicken's diet determines the color of the yolk. Chickens that eat mash and grains apparently lay eggs with yellow yolks. Chickens that eat mash and grains supplemented with grasshoppers, June bugs, sow bugs and earwigs lay eggs with orange yolks.

On the ranch we often got an egg with two yolks. This was the chicken equivalent of having twins. We called these eggs "double-yolkers," and they were a prize to find – like finding a four-leaf clover. I've never found a double-yolker in the ranch eggs we buy in the store. I think it's because the chicken-farm roosters don't measure up when compared to a real ranch rooster.

Sometime back in human history, somebody found out that chicken eggs were good for food. I'm not sure how this discovery was made because you could follow a chicken around for a long time before you'd find it laying anything worth eating. The chickens probably greeted this discovery with mixed feelings. From their perspective, the downside was that people were eating their kids, but the upside was that as long as people were eating eggs, the chance of their becoming fried chicken was diminished. As long as a chicken could keep laying eggs, it could avoid the frying pan. But eventually, when its productivity dropped off, its "retirement" would contribute a key ingredient in a recipe that Mom called *chicken croquettes*.

Chickens, like most other birds, like to lay their eggs in nests. When we had a chicken house, it had rows of nests. This was a fairly efficient system, but, like all ranches, things had a way of running down, wearing out and breaking. If you are the scientific type, you would recognize this phenomenon right away as the second law of thermodynamics, or entropy. All this means is that, left to themselves, things like ranches, cars, houses, people, chickens and chicken houses eventually run down, wear out and break down.

The point I'm making is that, as the chicken house aged and deteriorated, it provided opportunities for some of the chickens to escape. Eventually, they found a way to get over, under or around the fence that was supposed to keep them in. When this happened, they often came to realize too late that the fence intended to keep them in was also intended to keep the hawks and coyotes out. Natural selection ensures there are not many chickens that are both old and bold. Once a chicken is out of the "designated yard" and on the run, you are not likely to catch them again. This meant we had inside and outside chickens. The outside chickens still laid eggs, but it was a bit more difficult to find their nests.

By now, you have the drift: chickens lay eggs and people eat eggs, but in order to eat the eggs you had to participate in a chore called *collecting the eggs*. When we were young, this chore was usually delegated to Tom and me. Every other day or so, Mom would instruct us to collect the eggs, and we were off to accomplish this task.

Collecting eggs in the chicken house was not a real problem. All of the nests were in a row, and all we had to do was dislodge the chickens and gather up the eggs. Getting the chickens off the nests was not difficult. We simply walked into the chicken house, waved our arms and shouted "scat," and there would follow a crescendo of cackling, the beating of wings and a mighty rush of wind laden with dislodged feathers.

When the dust and feathers settled, the nests were clear of chickens, and we could collect the eggs. We had originally learned the word "scat" as a term to make cats disappear, but we found it worked equally well with chickens, especially if said loudly and accompanied with a lot of arm-waving. We have already established the sad fact that chickens are dumb, so they probably thought "scat" applied to them as well as cats.

Each nest usually had one to three eggs in it, and they were always warm – kept that way by a chicken who was never to be a mother. We usually put the eggs into a tin coffee can and, on a good day, we managed not to break any of them between the chicken house and the Red House. When we presented them to Mom, she counted them and praised us for the good job we had done.

The tricky part of collecting eggs was finding the ones laid by the outside (unconfined, or in yuppie language, free-range) chickens. The chickens that escaped the chicken yard laid their eggs in improvised nests in different places, and we had to find them wherever they might be. It was sort of like having an Easter-egg hunt every few days. The eggs weren't colored like Easter eggs, although they did come in brown and white.

One of the problems with finding an egg in a nest belonging to an outside chicken was that you didn't have any idea how old it was. If the chicken laid an egg and ended up coyote food, the egg might lie there several weeks before we found it. When we finally did find it, it could be quite rotten; but we wouldn't know until it was cracked open, which, of course, would immediately remove all doubt.

Rotten eggs smell so bad that they are the gold standard for things that smell bad. How often have you heard someone say that something smells as bad as rotten eggs? The possibility of collecting a rotten egg didn't appeal to Tom or me, so we found a way to deal with it. It all started out rather innocently, but I freely admit it got out of hand.

In order to determine whether an egg of unknown vintage was edible, we developed a foolproof *crack-n-sniff* quality control system. When we suspected the freshness of an egg, we cracked the shell and sniffed the egg. If it didn't smell right, we had done well; but if it smelled OK, we still had to find an alternate use for it because Mom didn't want us to bring home broken eggs.

It probably started when Tom threw a cracked egg at me rather than wasting it by tossing it in the weeds. No use destroying perfectly good ammunition. Of course I would have to retaliate the next time I cracked an egg, rotten or not. The next thing we knew, collecting eggs meant that we gathered some for food and some for ammunition for the inevitable egg fight. If we ran out of ammunition from the wild nests, we drew on our supply from the hen house.

As our enthusiasm for egg fights increased, Mom noticed that we were bringing home fewer and fewer eggs. We speculated with her as to all the reasons the chickens might be laying fewer eggs. Maybe the coyotes got some of the chickens? Perhaps a skunk had been stealing eggs? We had no end of suggestions, but Mom began to get suspicious pretty early on. It might have been the eggshells in our hair or the sticky yellow stains in the middle of our T-shirts. God apparently gives mothers ways of knowing things that remain a mystery to the rest of us.

"Have you boys been having egg fights?" she asked.

 "Do you mean us?"

"Yes, you. How did you get egg in your hair?"

"My hair? What egg?"

"You boys better jolly well tell me the truth!" Mom would say with a tone and look that meant the jig was up.

This would be the point where I had to give up my brother. "Tom started it. He threw an egg at me first, and all I did was defend myself."

"I did not. Chuck threw eggs too."

"Yeah, because you were throwing them at me first."

"No, sir."

"Yes, sir."

"I'm gonna get you."

"Mom! Tom's twisting my arm."

And so it was that collecting eggs led to egg fights resulting in shouting matches that deteriorated into arm-twisting battles that would come to an abrupt end when Mom threatened to "tan both your hides."

As we grew up on the ranch, any time Tom and I did chores together, we often managed to end up in some sort of rolling-on-the-ground fight. Whether collecting eggs, milking the cow, irrigating or chopping weeds, there was bound to be a battle in it somewhere. Being two years younger and smaller than Tom, I was in no danger of ever winning one of these scraps. From my perspective, a "good fight" was one that started near enough to the house so that Mom or Dad could hear me when I hollered for help. If that didn't work, I had to seek a truce by threatening to "tell" Mom or Dad when we got back to the house. Of course when I squealed on Tom, it was necessary to embellish the extent of the abuse to achieve the desired parental intervention and sympathy, but it's not like I had a lot of other options.

OFF WITH THEIR HEADS

It's probably no surprise to most people that chickens don't volunteer to become fried chicken. The process of moving a chicken from roost to roaster, or hatchet to skillet, is bound to ruffle some feathers. Chickens don't have much going for them, but they do have two useful attributes. First, chickens are "chicken." They are afraid of anything and everything. Second, they are dumb. If you are dumb as a stick, it's very handy to be timid at the same time. Being dumb and bold is a bad combination in any species, and I could cite any number of human examples from my career in law enforcement, but particularly so with chickens.

Being dumb is an important advantage to the chicken because their ignorance insulates them from the harsh reality of their lot in life (and death). There's a principle in life that most people learn but no chickens know until they meet their end. The principle is: There's no such thing as a free lunch. For a chicken, lunch is free until they become the lunch. When this happens, they have paid the price in full.

On the ranch, the first step in preparing a meal of fried chicken begins with catching the chicken. Mom would often send Tom and me to the chicken yard to grab dinner. Sometimes she specified a particular chicken, but most often she specified which ones not to catch. Of course the rooster was always off limits. Catching a chicken was a chore we didn't mind too much because it was the only time we could chase the chickens without getting into trouble.

Just because the chickens were in a pen, it didn't mean that catching one was going to be easy. None of them was going to volunteer to be caught, and all of the chickens were "chicken." They would run like crazy, and we had to chase them until we cornered one. Chickens on the run are not quiet. When you're trying to catch a single chicken, you end up with the whole flock running around, flapping their wings and squawking up a storm. In the commotion of all the running and flapping, a cloud of dust and feathers fills the air. The dust is normally about one part dirt and two parts dried chicken poop. This may be why Mom usually sent Tom and me to do the catching.

The chicken yard ambiance was no problem for us. A swirling atmosphere filled with squawks, dust, chicken poop and feathers was all part of what made chicken chasing fun. Eventually we would corner one and grab it. Sometimes a cornered chicken would go airborne and escape, but not often. Chickens are better fryers than flyers, but when motivated by the approach of two would-be chicken catchers, a really chicken chicken would sometimes go Peter Pan on us and fly the coop – temporarily.

Grabbing a chicken and controlling a chicken are two different things. A grabbed but uncontrolled chicken is a squawking, flopping, flapping, scratching, pecking machine. The trick is to hold the chicken by the legs with the wings secured against the legs. If done right, you can hold both legs and the tips of both wings with one hand. This traps the legs and wings, and keeps the pecking part of the chicken pointed away from you. Once secured this way, the chicken normally settles down, and you can transport it with minimal difficulty.

In the early years, Mom was the chief executioner. When Tom or I had caught and secured an appropriate chicken, we delivered it to Mom to receive the death penalty. This was accomplished by using a hatchet to chop off the chicken's head. For city kids, I may need to point out that it's necessary to kill the chicken before picking, cleaning and frying it. If you don't kill it first, it won't stand for the rest of the process. Put another way, you have to kill it to get it into the skillet.

We had a special stump that served as the official chopping block. The process was simple and straightforward. With the chicken in one hand and the hatchet in the other, the executioner positioned the chicken on the block and, with a swift *WHACK*, it was all over for that particular fowl. To be sure, it was not a pretty sight. The bloody chicken flopped around for a bit, but it was a necessary step if you wanted fried chicken.

When Tom and I got old enough so Mom trusted us with a hatchet, she sometimes had us deliver the *coup de grace*. We quickly found out that it was not quite as easy as Mom made it look. Properly done, the execution is accomplished with one quick whack. Improperly done – how should I put this? – it's messier, and the chicken gets really upset before it gets dead.

One time when Tom and I were still learning the craft, we apparently only managed to lop the top half of the head off. Chicken brains are really small, and you have to make sure they come off with the rest of the head. In this case we must have missed the brain because when we let go of the chicken, instead of flopping around and dying like a proper chicken, it stood up and started stumbling around. It didn't have a beak or eyes, and though the head appeared to be severed, the body was walking around, so the hatchet must have missed something vital. It took a second round at the chopping block to get the job done right.

Sometimes Mom would wring a chicken's neck before chopping its head off. She was really good at it, and with a quick spin, the chicken was dead and still, making it relatively easy to chop its head off. Tom and I tried this too but with considerably less success. We tried to imitate Mom's technique and spun it around by the neck a couple of extra times for good measure. However, when we let go, the chicken took off, and we had to catch it again. After you try to wring its neck, a chicken is much less likely to return to the block without putting up the fight of its life. Tom and I eventually gave up on wringing their necks and just went straight from catch it to hatchet.

CHICKEN PLUCKING

Once the chicken is dispatched, you are still a long way from the skillet, let alone the dinner table. Since they taste terrible, the next step in the process is to remove the feathers. This is a time-consuming procedure known as *chicken plucking*. It's accomplished by pulling out all of the feathers until the chicken is "naked."

Chicken plucking is a relatively low-skilled task, but there are some techniques that help expedite the procedure. Mom invariably recruited Tom and me to participate in the chicken plucking process, and it was not nearly as fun as chicken chasing.

Usually Mom dunked the chicken into boiling water before we started pulling off the feathers. This made the feathers come out easier, but wet chicken feathers smell worse than wet dog. Typically Mom tied twine around the chicken's legs and hung it upside down from a tree to make the picking easier. The feathers pull out easier when you pull toward the head – or in this case, where the head used to be. When the chicken was hanging upside down, all we had to do was pull down on the feathers and they came out fairly easily. Wet chicken feathers stick to your hands, so we had to shake the feathers off as we worked.

After most of the feathers were removed, we'd use a match to burn away the tiny little ones that remain when all the big ones are pulled out. For the record, burnt chicken feathers don't smell anything like fried chicken. Burnt chicken feathers smell worse than wet chicken and wet dog combined.

FINALLY – FRIED CHICKEN

When the chickens were plucked, Mom cleaned them and cut them into pieces that were just right for frying. The expression "clean the chickens" included washing them well, but it's also the polite term used for removing the gizzard and other uneatable inside parts of the chicken. This procedure is also known as "gutting," but the term "cleaning" is understandably more palatable.

As you can see, making fried chicken on the ranch was the end result of a lengthy process. When you get chicken at the supermarket, it has already been chased, caught, chopped, plucked, gutted, washed, cut and packaged. When you want fried chicken, all you have to do is buy it and fry it. But, if you ever find yourself in a situation where you need to make fried chicken from scratch, now you know "the rest of the fowl story."

CHAPTER EIGHT

MILKING THE COWS

Milking cows is an important part of ranch life. If you carefully studied the chapter about where milk *really* comes from, you should have a pretty good handle on the big picture involving ranchers, cows, bulls and milk. With this background, I think you are in a position to appreciate some of the particulars concerning that portion of the process known as *milking the cows*. In this chapter you'll learn details that will add color and dignity to a process that might otherwise seem to be nothing more than ruthless exploitation of the animal kingdom.

For most of my life on the ranch, we had a milk cow or two on hand. Before my brother Tom and I were old enough to milk the cows, we sometimes accompanied our father when he did the evening milking. During the winter it was almost always after dark by the time he got to the chore. While Dad was milking, Tom and I played on the bales of hay that were usually stacked high in the barn. It was cold, fun, dark and stickery. Sometimes we had flashlights to play with, but most of the time we played hide-and-seek in the dim light from the single light bulb in the corner of the barn where Dad was milking the cows.

Dad had an old electric radio that he plugged into the same socket that powered the light bulb. Battery-powered transistor radios were still waiting to be invented. The old radio rested on the sill just under the roof, and it was a raggedy thing without a case around it. When he turned the radio on, we could see the exposed tubes glowing in the dim light. Dad always listened to the radio while milking the cows. He said it settled the cows down, but I suspected it was just a way for a busy man to catch up on the news and to have some company in what was usually a big empty barn. It was a small luxury.

We had two cows on hand by the time Tom and I were old enough to start milking. We were assigned the chore as soon as we were big enough to sit on a stool and grip the applicable bovine appendages with enough strength to squeeze the milk out. The cow Tom milked was officially known as Patricia or Pat, but we always called her Bossy. The cow I milked was named Roamy, but for some reason she was usually called Goldie. On occasion, for reasons that will become obvious shortly, I called her "@#%&@#%."

You will recall that we normally only named animals we didn't intend to eat. Naming animals you intend to consume just complicates things. For example, most people like to eat steak or hamburger, but not too many would like to eat Chester or Happy, the Cow. If you don't plan to eat your cat, dog or milk cow, go ahead and name them; but don't name your food. It's a good rule of thumb.

Pat, the cow that Tom milked, was older, gentler and gave more milk than Goldie. Goldie was less cooperative and tended to be cranky. As the older son, Tom got to milk the kinder, gentler cow, and I got the ornery one – go figure. Among siblings, might makes right, and that is the sum of all the rules between big and little brothers.

Tom and I began milking when we were about 7 or 8 years old. We still lived in the old Red House when we started and continued after we moved to the new house on the ranch. We milked Pat and Goldie until they died. As a teenager, I came to intensely dislike the chore, but I swear that the cows died of natural causes, and nobody can prove otherwise. Anyway, old cows don't die, they just "kick the bucket" one time too many.

The cows were always milked in the large, wooden, creaky barn, which many years before had been painted red like the Red House. For some reason we didn't call it the Red Barn; we just called it "the barn." The schedule was relatively simple. We milked the cows in the morning before going to school, and we milked them again before going to bed. Cows didn't have days off, so neither did we. If Tom or I wanted to stay overnight with a friend, the other brother had to milk both cows, or sometimes Mom or Dad would stand in for the missing brother.

The cows were kept in an irrigated pasture just south of the Red House and west of the barn. Normally, as milking time approached, the cows could be found standing near the barn

THE BARN WHERE WE MILKED COWS.

door waiting for us to arrive. Our cows were golden-brown Guernseys, and they produced a lot of milk. Things got a bit "tight" and uncomfortable for them if we showed up late for the milking. If we were running unusually late, it was common to see milk spontaneously dribbling onto the ground beneath them. We always fed the cows hay and grain at milking time, so that gave them another incentive to look forward to our twice-daily visits. If the cows were feeling cantankerous, we had to go into the pasture and herd them to the barn, but that was the exception rather than the rule.

When we opened the barn door, the cows knew the routine. They walked right in and stuck their heads through the stanchions in their assigned stalls, where we had placed grain and hay for their dining pleasure. We locked them into their respective stalls by moving one of the upright boards of the stanchion lightly against their necks, where it was held in place by a locking block that dropped into place. Once locked in, they could move their head up and down, but they couldn't go forward or back out of the stall. It was necessary to lock them in because the milking process can take a while, and if the cow changes its mind about cooperating when you're in the middle of the procedure, things can get awkward. It's extremely difficult to milk a cow that's on the move, and, so far as I know, it's only done at rodeos.

Once the cow is locked in place and "manging" in the manger, we could go about the business of milking. The bovine milking appendages are located on the underside and toward the rear of the cow. They consist of a large udder from which four teats protrude. The job of milking is not finished until all four teats are dry, that is, until you cannot squeeze any more milk from the cow. The duration of the process depends upon the strength of your grip, the attitude of the cow, the attitude of the milker, whether the cow's calf escaped its pen and got to the cow's milk before you did, or whether you have a date later that night.

Normally the milking process takes from 10 to 15 minutes per cow, all things being equal. If you needed to get back to the house so you could clean up for a date, the milking could be accomplished in less than eight minutes, but with some slippage in quality control.

The job is accomplished while sitting on a low stool or, more often, an upside-down bucket so that your eyes and hands are at the appropriate level to engage the teats. After placing a clean bucket under the cow, you grasp two teats and pull down while squeezing at the same time. When done correctly, you can produce a substantial stream of milk. In practice, while you're using both hands, you usually only pull down on one teat at a time. While one hand is squeezing milk out of one teat, the other hand is repositioning its grip. With a bit of practice you can keep a steady stream flowing – left, right, left, right, left, right – and soon you learn how to fill the bucket without soaking your shoes.

MILKING COMPLICATIONS

A number of complications can slow down the milking process. One of the worst is when the cow has had a close encounter with a barbed-wire fence and has managed to cut one of her teats. When this would happen, it would still be my job to milk the cow, but it became the cow's job to avoid pain at all costs. These jobs are not compatible. After washing the injured appendage, we would apply a substance called Bag Balm to the affected area. Bag Balm seemed to soothe the injury somewhat and speeded healing. Still, milking a cow with a cut teat was a lot like tap dancing in a minefield. About every fourth or sixth squeeze (you never knew for sure), the cow would signal the presence of pain by kicking you, knocking over the bucket of milk or both. If you were standing just outside the barn door, it sounded something like this: *squirt, squirt, squirt, squirt, **kick**, slosh, clang, @#$%&@....squirt, squirt, squirt.*

Bag Balm was something of a universal miracle ointment on the ranch. We used it on ourselves as well as the cows, although not in the same places we applied it on the cows. Bag Balm doesn't smell particularly good, and it's a little greasy, but the whole family used it to help sooth and heal our cuts and bruises, or just to smooth rough hands. When you live on a ranch, your hands are usually a bit gnarly, and Bag Balm makes them soft again. I even keep Bag Balm around my house in the city. I used it to help heal a serious ankle injury I incurred in the line of duty as a police officer. Bag Balm comes in a square green can just like it did 50 years ago. It has a picture of a cow's head on the lid and a cow's udder on the side – but it works for me.

Another complication that could slow the milking process had to do with the particular location where the cow had slept during the previous eight hours. Cows are not really fussy when it comes to personal hygiene, and it is not uncommon for them to sleep on top of a fresh cowpie. As luck would have it, the affected area would be, as often as not, the udder or teats; or, worse, the location on the side of the cow where the milker's head would be pressed while milking.

If you haven't milked a cow with your face in near contact with the remains of a fresh cowpie, you haven't missed much. The bouquet leaves much to be desired, but in the event of inadvertent contact, you will find that it's an excellent hair treatment. Once it dries, it will keep your hair in place all day better than that green stuff barbers keep in a jar. Milking a cow with your face hovering near fresh cow poop can be done if you are very careful, but I wouldn't recommend it unless you are an experienced milker. It's better to clean off the cow crap first, though that takes a minute or two and extends the total time it takes to milk the cows. Somehow cows must know when you have a date or are otherwise in a hurry because they seem to roll in a large, fresh cowpie in advance nearly every time you're in a rush.

A particularly bothersome complication that slows down the milking process occurs during fly season. When it comes to cows, the fly season lasts from spring thaw until the first hard freeze. I don't think there's ever been a fly that met a cow it didn't like. It's not that the fly likes the cow's personality so much as it is that the cow's body makes a great socializing platform for flies when they are between cowpies. Most of the time the rear quarter of a cow is smeared with what we euphemistically called "guacamole," and the flies surely seemed to appreciate this. Presumably the guacamole was an ideal snack between cowpies.

The social relationship between cows and flies revolves around cowpies and is not particularly complex. When the cow deposits a "steamer" in the pasture, the flies quickly abandon the cow for a mating and feeding frenzy on the surface of the fresh cowpie. The relationship between cows and flies is sort of like the relationship between kids and an ice cream truck, except the cow's product is hot rather than cold, it only comes in chocolate and it's free. I guess the analogy deteriorates rapidly, but the point is that flies tend to congregate around cows, and kids gather around ice cream trucks – and we'll leave it at that.

The problem with flies and cows is that during fly season, the cow is always transporting a few hundred flies wherever it goes. Cows are not particularly sensitive, but they do notice it when flies take off and land on their backs, especially if the fly is somewhat clumsy about it. The flies crawl around on the cow; some bite and that also adds to the cow's irritation. Cows respond to fly irritation by employing their built-in fly swatter. A cow's tail ends with a lot of long hairs, sort of like a frayed rope, and it makes an excellent fly swatter. From where the tail is attached on the north end of a southbound cow, it can swat flies at least halfway up the body toward the head. If the cow is so inclined, it can swing its head back and chase flies off of the forward portion of the body. The tail and head operating in concert make the cow a pretty effective fly-swatting machine.

But when we were milking, the cow's head was secured in the stanchion, and this put half of the cow's fly-swatting system out of commission. It also meant that the fly irritation factor was increased by 50 percent while we were engaged in the process of milking the cow. To compensate for the increased discomfort, the cow's brain sends a message to the tail instructing the tail to double its switching output. This is just fine for the cow, but it's bad for the flies, and it's really bad for the kid milking the cow. Cow tail switching is not a precise science; in fact it's downright indiscriminate. The milker and the flies both get swatted on a regular basis.

Getting swiped across the face by the frayed rope attached to the cow's butt stings, but that is not really the worst part. The worst part relates to where the cow's fly swatter attaches to the cow. The proximity of the cow's fly swatter to the cow-pie delivery system ensures that the tail is usually coated with guacamole. That's the worst part. A guacamole-coated fly swatter stings more than a dry one. I'm not saying the cow does it on purpose, but a well aimed swish can wrap that tail around your head twice, with the guacamole-coated tip ending up in your mouth. You just can't spit enough when that happens.

Another complication that interferes with the milking process is when the cow kicks the bucket over or puts her foot in the bucket. Out of necessity, we developed procedures to handle each of these contingencies.

Cows will, on occasion, kick over the bucket. For some reason, this normally happens when you are almost done so that the maximum quantity of the milk is lost. The reasons cows kick over buckets can vary. Most often they are trying to kick you, and they simply miss and hit the bucket by accident. However, it could be because they are just shifting their feet or reacting to an itch. An experienced milker develops good reflexes and can see a lot of the kicks coming in time to grab the bucket and save the milk. But it's not possible to be 100 percent effective in this, so you have to expect to lose a bucket of milk from time to time.

Mom didn't like it when we came back from the barn with only half the usual milk because one of the cows had kicked over the bucket. When this happened, we normally got a "be more careful" lecture, so we did our best to save the milk to avoid the lecture. With any luck we could literally squeeze more milk out of the cow after she kicked the bucket over, so we would have something to show for our time and effort. If we could deliver *some* milk, this also shortened Mom's lecture.

When the cow puts her foot *in* the bucket, it's a different situation. The reason cows occasionally put a foot in the milk bucket varies, but mostly it's just because they're stupid. After they try to kick you or a cat, they have to put their foot somewhere, so it might as well be in the milk bucket. It doesn't seem to matter one way or another to the cow.

When this happens, your first challenge is to get the cow to lift her foot out of the bucket. Cows are not particularly agile and not particularly motivated to raise their feet high enough to clear the top of the bucket. I guess the foot feels warm and toasty in the milk, so the clumsy cow figures, "Why move it?"

So far as I know there's no method sanctioned by the People for Ethical Treatment of Animals to get a cow to lift her foot out of the bucket. Pleading, hollering and waving our arms had no noticeable effect, so we'd slap the cow on the butt and push on her until she lifted her leg and we could grab the bucket. As often as not, the milk was spilled in the process. This meant that we had to tell Mom that the cow kicked over the bucket and subject ourselves to another "be more careful" scolding.

If the cow managed to lift her leg out of the bucket without spilling it, I had two options. I could, and admittedly should, consider the milk contaminated and throw it away, but then I would have to defend myself to Mom. On the other hand, if, upon inspection, the cow's foot didn't have as much crap on it as it usually did, I could consider the milk "salvageable." All I had to do was add a second filter to the strainer through which I poured the milk to bottle it, and I could rationalize that it was completely sanitized. Of course I myself wouldn't drink any milk until that batch was gone, but I figured what the rest of the family didn't know wouldn't hurt them. The important thing at the time was to avoid the "be more careful" lecture. In the process, it's entirely possible that the Nelson family developed antibodies to diseases that medical science has yet to discover.

BARN CATS AND MILKING COWS

Among the skills you develop when milking cows is the ability to squirt far and to squirt accurately. The digital dexterity and muscularity you develop with twice-daily cow milking cannot be underestimated. Such skill cannot go unexercised and undemonstrated.

An accurate squirt of 10 to 15 feet from the cow is no problem for the expert. All that is needed is an appropriate target. The most common and abundant targets were cats. Cats and milk are a natural combination.

We always had an abundance of cats around the barn. We only had female cats, but apparently male cats employed as itinerant inseminators traveled through the area to service them at regular intervals because they were pregnant with monotonous regularity.

With cats and kittens in abundance, we usually had a target-rich environment at milking time. As a diversion and to test our skills, we would regularly squirt cats or kittens as they wandered within squirt range. The cat's typical initial reaction was surprise followed by flight. However, as some of the cats got used to it, they would sit still and let you squirt milk right into their mouths. They would "chew" on the stream of milk as it went into their mouths and splattered all over their fur. They ended up a dripping, sticky, wet mess of milk-soaked fur.

The ubiquitous cats did, on occasion, complicate the milking operation. When milking the cows, you were generally located toward the center of a moving constellation of cats and kittens. When you weren't using them for target practice, you had to occasionally push them away from the cow's feet. On one occasion Tom reported that Bossy set her foot down on top of a kitten, creating a permanently flat cat. It's sad to think about now, but at the time, we were not experiencing a cat shortage.

Another cat-related problem could arise when a cat walked under the cow with its tail sticking straight up. Cats get all happy when they think you're going to give them some milk, and when a cat is happy, it walks around twitching its tail in the air. When the twitching cat's tail contacts the sensitive underside of a cow, it apparently triggers some sort of primitive bovine reflex. The cow becomes agitated, probably figuring it's under attack, and reflexively kicks in the direction of the tickle. Unfortunately, the milk bucket is situated between the cow's kicker and the tickle, so sometimes the milk would be knocked over or the cow's foot ended up in the milk.

When the milking was done and we were leaving the barn, we always paused to pour some milk into a pan we kept on the barn floor. As soon as we did this, a considerable herd of cats descended on the pan. Soon the pan was ringed with furry heads toward the center and happy twitching tails to the outside.

ACCOMMODATING VISITORS WHILE MILKING COWS

When relatives and city friends came to visit us on the ranch, they often liked to come with us when we went to milk the cows. What was a daily chore for us was a novelty for them, and they liked to watch the operation. Usually visitors were impressed by such mundane things as the number of flies on the cows, how much guacamole the cow had accumulated on its hind quarter or how bad the barnyard smelled.

Some visitors actually liked warm milk fresh from the cow. We would milk right into a clean glass so they could enjoy milk as fresh as it can be. Others were fascinated by the process and asked lots of questions, which we answered as we worked. The best part of having visitors was the entertainment they provided when we squirted them with fresh, warm milk. The trick was to lure them into range and position without raising their suspicions. The ones who had been squirted before were the hardest to deceive. The objective was to try to squirt them in the face, preferably the mouth, as they were talking. My favorite shot was when I squirted a girl in the mouth at the precise moment she was articulating the word "trap." I awarded myself extra points for that accomplishment.

The more experienced friends and relatives stopped visiting us at milking time. They stayed at the house or at least stayed out of the barn while we were milking. That was OK too.

RIDING THE CALF

While we were down at the barn milking the cows, there were other ways to entertain ourselves, such as playing rodeo by trying to ride the year-old calves. We would herd them into the barn and close the door behind them. Then I would climb up on a calf, and Tom would throw the barn door open and whack the calf on the butt. What followed was usually a short, bumpy ride that ended with me on the ground.

Because the rides always concluded with me on my back in the barnyard, this was mostly a winter sport. In the winter I was normally bundled up in a thick, oversized Army-surplus parka that helped cushion the landing. More important, during the winter the barnyard was generally covered with at least 6 to 8 inches of pliable mud and cow crap. This surface was far more effective than the parka in cushioning a fall. If the barnyard mud and crap was frozen rock-solid, we held off on calf riding until the next thaw.

As for the parka, it eventually became coated with barnyard goo and gained a personality of its own. I had to hang it in the woodshed because Mom wouldn't let it in the house. I really liked that coat. It was warm, and since nobody else seemed to want to get near it, I could wear it whenever I wanted.

My calf-riding enthusiasm dwindled somewhat after I was launched forward over a calf's head and got whacked in the face by its nubbin horns as I went by. I had a huge raspberry on the side of my face, and my jaw was sore for weeks.

THE SEPARATOR

Each morning and evening after we milked the cows, rode the calf, had an egg fight and accomplished other daily rituals, we had to process the milk. This involved pouring some of the milk into quart and gallon glass jars that we used for our home milk supply.

First we poured the milk through a filter/strainer that was mounted in the bottom of a large stainless steel funnel. The filter was made of paper or, if we ran out of store-bought filters, we used cloth, usually a clean handkerchief. The milk went from the strainer into the jars.

The milk we didn't bottle for home use went into the "separator." A separator is a device that divides whole milk into skimmed milk and cream. It consists of a lot of stainless steel parts that we had to wash twice a day after milking the cows. We poured the whole milk through the strainer into a large stainless steel bowl at the top of the separator. The milk then ran down through a hole in the center into a spinning set of cones with holes in them. As the milk flowed through the spinning cone set, centrifugal force separated the cream from the milk. The cream was directed out one spigot, while the skimmed milk flowed out of another. We caught the cream in a jar or stainless steel canister and the skimmed milk in a bucket.

We used the cream for cooking, to make butter and sometimes to make homemade ice cream. Usually we had enough extra cream to sell to neighbors or the local creamery. The skimmed milk was usually fed to the pigs unless Mom wanted it for cooking or to make cottage cheese.

The heart of the separator was the spinning-cone device. When we first moved onto the ranch, we had to turn a hand-crank to spin the separator. This was hard work. Later, Dad bought an electric separator, which made processing the milk much easier and faster.

HOME DAIRY PRODUCTS

Since we had milk from our own cows, we seldom bought milk from the store. Unlike store-bought milk, our milk was not homogenized or pasteurized. When the milk sat in the refrigerator, the cream would float to the top. Before we put it on the table at dinnertime, we had to tighten the lid and shake the jar vigorously to homogenize the cream and milk. Our milk was far richer than anything you could buy in a store.

Our cream was thick and made great whipped cream, butter and ice cream. I remember my father telling my mother that he would eat anything with homemade whipped cream on it. Mom threatened to put it on a cowpie to see if he would back up his words, but she never got around to it.

Churning butter was one of the chores that often fell to me. I would complain when it was my turn, but I really didn't mind it. Our churn was a large square jar into which a wooden paddle extended. The paddle was attached to a gear assembly on the lid and was turned by a crank that extended from the lid assembly.

Mom filled the churn with cream, and I started turning the crank. The cream sloshed around in the square jar, and it took quite a while for it to start to congeal into butter. Eventually I would see deep yellow-gold chunks swirling around in the cream. As I kept churning, the chunks became more numerous, and the churning got more and more difficult. Finally, I was through.

Mom poured off the remaining fluid, which was usually nothing more than pale blue-white milk. In the bottom of the churn was a large clump of yellow-gold nuggets of butter. Mom added a bit of salt to the butter nuggets. Then she'd use a wooden paddle to work the butter into a round wooden butter mold. The butter was pressed firmly into the mold until it filled the mold completely. Then, with a handle that extended from the top of the mold, she'd push the round cylinder of rich yellow-gold butter from the mold. The top of the mold had a leaf-shaped pattern carved into it, so the butter that emerged from the mold was topped with this leaf pattern.

The butter on our table at the ranch didn't look at all like the familiar pale-yellow cubes we see today. Store-bought butter pales in both color and taste by comparison to our rich, golden homemade butter on the ranch. I guess, as with so many things in life, the best butter comes from churning it yourself.

Sometimes we made homemade ice cream. This was also better than anything you could buy in a store, but it required a lot of ice and a lot of cranking. Sometimes Mom would flavor our homemade ice cream with fresh blackberries. Most of the time we bought ice cream from the creameries in Grenada or Montague where we sold our extra cream. Their ice cream was almost as good as homemade.

CLOSING THOUGHTS ABOUT MILKING

Milking the cows was a chore to be sure, but it wasn't all that bad. Like most things in life, it's more fun to look back on milking the cows than actually doing it. We had to milk the cows when it was hot and when it was cold. During the summer we usually milked after sunrise and before sunset, but during the shorter winter days, it was often done in the dark. We milked cows when it rained and when it snowed, but we were in the barn so we didn't suffer that much during the actual milking.

During the winter the barn creaked and groaned as the wind whistled and howled outside and pushed icy air through the cracks in the walls. On dark, windy winter nights, the light bulb that was our sole source of light would swing in the wind, sending spooky shadows throughout the barn. At such times I was glad to be milking the cows with my big brother for company.

I remember how fast I could milk the cows when I had some-place to go in the evening. I remember sleepily milking the cows early in the morning before catching the bus for school. It was a twice-daily chore, part of my life, for many years.

One of my most nostalgic memories associated with milking dates back to my teenage years. After dark on a cold winter

AS IT STOOD IN 2004, THE BARN WHERE WE ONCE MILKED COWS, PLAYED IN THE HAY AND PRACTICED OUR RODEO SKILLS WAS A BATTERED REMNANT OF BYGONE DAYS.

night, Tom and I were driving a beat-up pickup from the barn up to the house after milking the cows. It was country dark beyond the reach of the pickup's headlights, but as we got near the house we could see the Christmas tree in the living room window. This is one of the vivid memories that has stuck with me through the years, the welcoming sight of a warm ranch house and the colorful lights of Christmas shining through the cold black winter night at the end of a muddy dirt road.

CHAPTER NINE

ALL ABOUT CATTLE

The most appropriate use of the term *ranch* is in reference to a reasonably large piece of property where cattle are raised, a *cattle ranch*. I have occasionally encountered people who claim to have grown up on a ranch, but after a little discussion, it turns out that they lived on a place where fruits or nuts were raised. In my book (and this is my book, so I guess I can set the rules), if you're all hat and no cattle, you don't have a ranch.

Who the heck ever heard of a kumquat ranch? When do you round up the apricots or brand the walnuts? In addition to lacking cattle, some of these fruit and nut "ranches" are limited to a few hundred acres or less. Face it folks, these are orchards. Few people evidently want to admit they grew up on an orchard, so they say they grew up on a ranch. I suppose you can't blame them, but, for the record, a *proper* ranch needs cattle.

Since the term *cattle* is an important part of the definition of a ranch, I should define *cattle* for those of you who grew up in the city or a fig orchard. In general use, you can substitute the term *cattle* for *cows*. If you see a bunch of cows in a field, you can say, "Look at the cattle." This is an acceptable usage of *cattle*, but it's not entirely accurate.

Cattle generally refers to domesticated mammals of the genus *Bos* (bovines). The term *cow* usually refers to adult females, while *bulls* are uncastrated adult male bovines. Bulls and cows are cattle, and so are *steers* (castrated bulls) and *heifers* (young cows). If your ranch includes a number of cows, bulls, heifers, steers and calves, you have a genuine cattle ranch. If your ranch consists of walnuts, figs and apricots, you have a genuine orchard, so get used to it.

HERDING CATTLE

A bunch of cattle in a field is called a *herd* of cattle. The process of moving cattle from one field into another, or from place to place, is called *herding the cattle*. It can also be called a *cattle drive*, though I've never seen cattle drive anywhere – they generally walk in herds. Depending on circumstances, you can herd cattle on foot, on horseback or in a vehicle. My favorite way of herding cattle was on a motorcycle, but most of my herding was done as a kid on foot and with my father on a horse. Herding cattle is not rocket science, but there are a few "does and don'ts" to keep in mind. We learned most of the "does" by doing the "don'ts" first.

MOVING THE HERD TOWARD NUMBER 4 FIELD.

In the summer months, when the cattle were grazing in the irrigated pastures, we had to periodically rotate them between fields. When the cattle eat the grass down in one field, they must be rotated into another field so the grass can grow back again. During the summer growing season, a rotation system is established to move the cattle from field to field as the grass is eaten down in one and grows back in another. In order to keep the pastures green and growing, we had to continually irrigate them. During the summer, cattle ranching is largely a matter of keeping the pastures green and growing, and the cattle fed and happy. It's not a complicated system, but it works.

We had to herd the cattle from one field to another every so many days or weeks depending on the size of the field and size of the herd. The larger the herd or the smaller the field, the less time it took the cattle to eat the grass down. (I believe I mentioned that this isn't rocket science.)

When we moved the cattle into a ready-to-eat field, they just loved to wade out into tall green grass and graze away. Sometimes I wondered what it would be like to be a cow standing in a field surrounded with delicious food. Would it be like a human standing knee-deep in a 60-acre pizza? The cattle seemed to relish their green grass as much as any person ever enjoyed a pepperoni pizza. However, you don't want to take this analogy too far because green grass passes through a cow and ends up as a cowpie, which is deposited on top of the grass the cow will eat later on. This troubling fact reveals the shortcoming of the pizza analogy and a key difference between the dining habits of cattle and people.

Cattle may be stupid, but they know when they are out of food. Cattle are regular eating machines, and when the food is gone, they get restless. Once they eat the grass down in one field, they know the rancher is supposed to do something about it. If the next pasture in the rotation system is an adjacent field, all the rancher has to do is to open the gates between the fields, and the cattle, with relatively little assistance, can figure out that it would be a good thing to go from the field without any food to a new field with lots of food. Accordingly, they move through the gate and essentially herd themselves into the new field without a great deal of effort on the rancher's part.

If the rancher is tardy in getting around to moving the cattle after the grass is gone in a field, the cattle will sometimes get restless enough to move themselves. They accomplish this by tearing the fence down, and in the process some of them usually manage to cut themselves up a bit. The fences are barbed wire, which normally discourages self-moving, but sometimes cattle will initiate a freelance move that involves walking through a barbed wire fence. The cuts they endure heal soon enough and are just part of the price of being stupid. To avoid fence and cattle repair problems, ranchers usually find it expedient to move the cattle in a timely fashion when the feed gets low.

We identified the various irrigated pastures on the ranch by numbers. Ultimately we had eight irrigated fields, so we had Fields Nos. 1 through 8. Field No. 1 was near the Red House, and Field No. 8 was out in the northwest section of the ranch. Moving the cattle between fields was not too difficult if the fields were adjacent or connected. The problems came when we had to herd the cattle some distance, especially if we had to move them over dry land to get them to the next irrigated pasture. For example, if we had to move the cattle from No. 1 to No. 5, we had to herd them overland, and this was when difficulties would sometimes arise.

When we were kids, Dad would call on us to help with the difficult moves. As a kid I was always a bit nervous around cattle because they were a lot larger than I was, and there were many more of them than there was of me. This meant that I didn't enter into the herding process with confidence.

The second reason I was nervous was because I knew exactly what was going to go wrong.

The first step of the move involved opening the gate we wanted the cattle to use to enter the new field. Next we opened the gate we wanted the cattle to use to exit the field they were currently occupying. At this point, Dad would give Tom and me instructions that would consist of pointing to a distant part of the field and saying something like, "Stand over there, and when I herd the cattle toward you, head them toward the gate, but don't crowd them and don't let any of them get around you."

I remember watching carefully where Dad had pointed because I knew it was going to be critical to stand exactly in the spot he designated. These instructions would be given in a firm but calm speaking voice, and they would be the last even-tempered words we would hear from Dad for the next several hours. From this time forward, Dad's herding instructions would consist of angry shouts and vigorous gestures, accompanied by some remarkably imaginative and descriptive cussing.

The herding process began when Dad rode his horse out into the field and started working the cattle toward the open gate. Tom and I were usually on foot and located on either side of the gate, but well back from it. Our

SEDG ON "BUD" – BRINGING UP A STRAGGLER.

119

job was to keep the cattle headed toward the gate without letting any of them drift off to either side.

If a cow got past us, Dad cussed and hollered; if we were too close to the herd, Dad cussed and hollered; and if we were too far back, Dad cussed and hollered. We had to be in exactly the right place to avoid the cussing and hollering, and I never could find that place as hard as I tried. I didn't realize until I was an adult that there was no magic place I could have stood to avoid his wrath. Anger was Dad's default setting when we were herding the cattle.

When the herd got to the open gate, they invariably balked for a while and bunched up without going through the gate. Who knows why? It's just a cow thing. The cattle in the front could see the open gate but instead of going through it, they would sniff the air, then sniff the ground, then sniff the gate and the nearest fence post, then sniff another cow's butt, then make a cowpie. In the meantime the rest of the herd was bunching up behind their aimless leaders. But the back of the herd couldn't see the open gate; all they could see was cattle butts in front of them.

For some reason, it was constantly a problem to entice the first cattle through an open gate. This was always a tense time because when the cattle have people on each side and behind them, and a fence in front of them (even with an open gate), they are likely to do something stupid.

As cattle herders, our objective at this point was to make sure we didn't get too close or hang back too far. If we got too close, we could cause the cattle to panic, which might incite them either to tear the fence down or to explode in 150 different directions. As you might imagine, it's difficult to surround a herd of cattle running in 150 different directions with three people. If we held back too far, the cattle would turn around and start walking away from the gate or decide to try an end run on us. To keep Tom and me from getting too close or too far back, Dad hollered "colorful" instructions that intimidated us, the cattle and the horse he was riding.

Finally, after what seemed like an eternity, a few cattle walked timidly through the open gate and others would begin to fall in line. Cattle tend to be followers rather than independent thinkers, so as soon as one or two start moving in a direction, the others usually join the parade. As the cattle started going through the gate, the back of the herd, the ones that couldn't see anything but cow butts, detected the movement and started pushing ahead. When the cattle started moving through the gate, we would close in on them to encourage them to continue their progress. However, we still had to make sure we didn't crowd them because if we got too close, they could still panic and do something stupid. If I haven't mentioned it, stupid is the default setting for cattle, but they can alternate between stupidity and panic in an instant.

If things were going well for us and we got all the cattle through the gate without incident, we then had to herd the cattle overland to the field we wanted to put them in. This was not usually too much of a problem because in the open range, as long as the lead cattle are headed in the right direction, the rest will follow. Tom and I ran along behind and on the sides of the herd, keeping them bunched and headed in the right direction and keeping the mavericks in line. Dad followed on his horse, occasionally galloping ahead to make sure the herd was heading in the right direction. This was the relatively easy part of herding the cattle. The real problem lay ahead of us.

Herding cattle is a noisy business – even apart from the hollering and cussing. When cattle are being herded, they make a lot of noise. Cows moo to keep in touch with their calves, calves moo to keep in touch with their mothers and all the others moo because that's what cows do when they're engaged in any activity except eating. Dad, Tom and I would also be whistling and hollering (trying to sound like John Wayne) and waving our arms as necessary to keep the cattle on target.

If you were to listen to a cattle drive, it would sound something like this: **MOOOOOOOOO** (that's a cow); **HEY-AAAAAAAA** (that's a cowboy); **MBAAAAA** (that's a calf, we didn't mix sheep with the cattle); **HUP, HUP, HUP** (another cowboy); **MOOOOOOO** (another cow); **@#$%@$%#** (adult cowboy); **MOOOMOOOOOOO** (two cows at the same time); *MBAAAAAAA (How'd that sheep get in here?);* **HEYAAAAAAAAA, tweeeeeeeet** (cowboy).

In addition to the noise, herding cattle produces a lot of dust, especially when you are out of the irrigated pasture and herding cattle overland. Herding cattle involves all of your senses. Mixed in with the mooing, hollering, whistling and dust is the "bouquet" of the herd. Cattle get nervous when they are being herded, and anxious cattle poop a lot. Nervous cow poop is runnier than calm cow poop, and a walking cow doesn't produce the same classic, circular cowpie that a cow at rest emits. The walking cowpie tends to be longitudinally deformed and covers much more surface area. It's likely to cover grass and sagebrush up to knee height, and rocks can become slippery. When herding cattle, you don't want to wear your best clothes or shoes.

SEDG NELSON ON "BUD" IN NO. 5 FIELD.

The next tricky part of the move was getting the cattle through the gate leading into the new field. This involved herding the cattle up against a fence with an open gate in it, just as we did a short time before when we moved them out of the old field. However, for some inscrutable reason, especially given the cows' very recent experience with filing through an open gate, this part never went smoothly. The herd always bunched up and balked before going through the open gate.

When this happened, Tom and I would search desperately for the place to stand that wasn't too close or too far back from the herd to earn us a burst of Dad's verbal thunder. Yet, when the lead cows finally went through the open gate and the herd began to follow, we knew the worst was yet to come.

The first ones through the gate invariably stopped to graze, or to admire the view or just to revel in their own stupidity. The rest of the herd, having sensed a bit of forward progress, started moving through the gate but had to come to a stop because the cattle in front of them were blocking the way. The back of the herd knew something was happening but couldn't see anything but cow butts, so they got nervous and frustrated.

At this point some of them would turn around and stare wild-eyed at Tom, Dad and me behind them. They were nervous about being herded, they couldn't go forward through the sea of cow butts, and when they turned around, there were these raggedy looking cowboys behind them. Where were they to go? What were they to do? This is tough stuff for a cow brain to figure out, so they tended to skip the thinking part and went straight to panic.

Dad would be cussing, waving his arms and ordering Tom and me to move up here and move back there. **"DON'T @#%$ CROWD THEM, GET $@% BACK OVER THERE, @&%@#. NO, NOT THERE, I SAID GO BACK! WHERE THE $@#@$&# ARE YOU GOING?"** By this time, Tom and I probably looked as wild-eyed as the spooked cattle at the back of the herd.

Then, after bunching up at the gate, the herd would suddenly start pushing rapidly through the gate into the new field. With a thunder of hooves, a chorus of bellowing and a cloud of dust, the entire herd tried to go through the gate at the same time. Since the entire herd couldn't fit through the gate simultaneously, the fence would often be knocked over. Dad always got a little extra upset when the cattle knocked the fence down, and you could clearly hear his cussing over the clamor of the herd.

Then it happened. From out of the cloud of dust, a frenzied cow would come thundering right at us. In the noise, confusion and dust, at least one cow, high on panic and low on IQ, would get turned around and make a break for it. We'd jump, shout and wave our arms to try to turn it back, but it would run between us and hightail it for the farthest reaches of the ranch. Dad would gallop after it with his horse farting and his mouth trailing a stream of scorching profanity that withered the grass for 20 feet on either side of him.

If you've ever been around horses, you know they fart a lot. They especially fart when you run them, but they fart when you walk them and they fart when they're standing still. If you have two horses, they'll fart a duet. I never could figure out how Hollywood made all those cowboy movies without detectable horse farting. I figured it was something like trick photography, or they just did a lot of retakes. Horses are the reason I like to herd cattle on foot or on a motorcycle. Motorcycles are easier to catch when you want to go for a ride, and they don't fart.

And so it was that herding the cattle on the ranch was usually a two-hour ordeal. Thirty minutes of the process went into moving the herd from one field to another, and one and a half hours were required to run down that last panicked cow that wouldn't go through the gate and to repair the fences. Whatever the circumstances, I always understood that the fault for an escapee cow was mine because I wasn't standing in the right spot. I never minded the noise, dust, slippery rocks and aroma of the herd, but I always dreaded the angry cussing that was part of herding cattle.

I realize that I haven't provided a particularly flattering portrayal of my father in this description of a cattle drive. He was an exacting person with a short fuse, and the emotion he seemed most comfortable in sharing with others was anger. He appeared gracious from a distance but was tough on anyone who got close to him. I suppose it was inevitable that he would spend his last days alone on the ranch at the end of his life.

As an adult I came to understand many of the dynamics of his early life that shaped the person he became. While I deeply regret his anger and our inability to have a closer relationship, I am grateful that he provided for our material needs, and I'm thankful for the many good lessons he taught us along the way. All of his sons have a work ethic that has served us well. Dad often said, "Any job worth doing is worth doing well." Usually this advice was followed up with, "So get back out there and do it right."

WINTERING CATTLE

When the cold months came, the irrigated pastures stopped growing and turned from summer green to winter brown. We didn't have to irrigate during the winter, but we still had to look after the cattle.

In the fall we moved the cattle out of the irrigated fields and onto the rangeland. The rangeland usually had enough wild grass to feed the cattle for several weeks before we

WINTER FEEDING ON THE NORTH RANGE.

had to start hauling hay to sustain them through the winter months.

Most years Dad used all of the pastureland for grazing cattle rather than growing alfalfa for hay. Consequently, we had to buy hay to get the cattle through the winter. Since this was a significant expense, Dad sold all the cattle he planned to sell before winter set in. This way he only had to feed the core of the herd through the winter. The core of the herd consisted of pregnant cows, a few bulls and a few replacement heifers. Any cow that didn't manage to get pregnant got sold – no use paying to fuel an empty truck.

When snow fell and covered the range grass, the cattle relied entirely on hay for food, so hauling hay to the herd was a daily chore. Dad had a large pickup that we loaded with hay and drove out to a flat area on the range to feed the cattle.

A TYPICAL LINE OF CATTLE FEEDING ON HAY THROWN FROM THE BACK OF THE PICKUP.

With the pickup in low gear and moving slowly, someone would climb on top of the hay, cut the wire or twine on the bales, and start throwing the hay down to the cattle that followed along behind the truck. You didn't want to put all the hay in one place because then only a small number of cattle could get at it. By spreading it out over a large area, all the cattle had access to the hay without trampling it.

"Haying the cattle" was best done as a two-man job, but typically Dad or his hired hand did it alone. When his sons were grown up and gone, Dad often had a hired hand to help him with ranch work, including feeding the cattle. A ranch constantly has something that needs fixing or a project that needs to be completed, so there's always work enough for two people. When the hired hand took his days off, Dad did the feeding by himself. Ranch work is never done. (See Appendix A).

When one person fed the cattle, the first step was to load the pickup high with hay from the barn. The amount of hay delivered was based on estimating a certain number of pounds of hay per cow. This amount could be adjusted depending on whether there was any range grass available to supplement their feed and how healthy the herd looked. Hay is expensive and not to be wasted, but the cattle need to be kept healthy.

As soon as the cattle saw the pickup coming, they would start heading toward it. Sometimes the driver would blow the pickup's horn to attract any cattle that were out of sight. Cattle are not bright, but they know when it's time to eat, and they know what a truckload of hay is all about.

When he'd found an appropriate flat spot, the driver would put the pickup in low gear and let the engine idle. The idle speed was set so that the pickup would creep forward without requiring pressure on the gas pedal. (Kids, please don't try this at home.) While the pickup was crawling forward, the driver would climb out of the cab and up on top of the truck and start throwing hay down to the cattle that were following behind. He would keep an eye on where the pickup was headed, and if he saw it was headed for a hole or a rock, he would either climb back into the cab and steer around it, or shut off the engine with a kill switch that had been rigged on top of the cab.

FEEDING THE BULLS.

During the winter we also had to make sure the cattle had water to drink. It was never a problem during the summer because the cows were in the pastures and there was always water in the irrigation ditches. In the winter the cattle on the range near the river always had water because the river never froze over. However, sometimes the cattle had to get their water from a watering trough or the lake.

When it got really cold, it was always a problem to keep the water flowing into the troughs because the lines or faucets tended to freeze. When the water in the watering trough was frozen over, the cattle couldn't drink, so we would use an ax to break up the ice. After breaking the ice, we used a pitchfork to throw the large chunks out of the trough so the cattle would have a few hours' access to the water before it froze over again.

When Dad was feeding the cattle in the winter, he was always accompanied by one or more ranch dogs. One of the dogs liked to lie on the hood of the pickup above the heat from the motor. It was quite a sight: a pickup piled high with hay chugging along through frozen ruts with a rangy old ranch dog lying on the hood. Dad had to peer through a frosted windshield and around a large canine hood ornament to see where he was going.

ROUNDUP

With cattle, as with chickens and people, there's no such thing as a free lunch. Ranchers raise cattle, not because they make good pets, but for food and profit. Like plumbing, accounting and carpentry, ranching is a way to make a living. It's a job, a way to put clothes

SEDG AND HIRED HAND "ROUND UP" A RECALCITRANT CALF.

on your back, food on your table and a roof over your head. It's different from a lot of other jobs because a good rancher also has to serve as his own accountant, plumber, carpenter and mechanic – not to mention veterinarian and chief executive officer. Ranching is a business, and cattle are a product. This is an uncomfortable concept for those with romantic notions about the ranching lifestyle, but it is, nevertheless, reality.

PUSHING CALVES INTO THE CROWDING PEN.

The rancher buys or rents bulls to keep the cows pregnant, so they will have calves, so the rancher will have cattle to sell, so he can buy stuff for his family. As with milk cows and chickens, the rancher has a certain emotional relationship with his cattle, but it's not always pretty.

Now that we've dispelled any romantic notions about the cattle business, this is a good time to talk about the *round-up*. This is when the cattle are herded into the corral and "processed."

The first roundup activity is the branding. New calves that have not yet been branded must be marked for identification. Cattle are mobile, fences aren't foolproof and this can sometimes lead to problems. One type of problematic mobility is called *straying*. If a cow escapes your ranch by going through a fence or swimming across the river, it's called straying. A stray cow can end up joining another rancher's herd and, without a brand, it would be difficult to tell who owns which cow.

Another inappropriate form of cattle mobility is called *rustling*. This is when a bad guy steals one or more of your cattle; it's cow theft. Rustling is a bad thing because a cow thief is stealing the rancher's livelihood. In the olden days, ranchers used to hang rustlers, but now they just go to jail or prison (or to therapy if they get a lenient judge). Branding cattle is sort of like putting a license plate on your car; it discourages rustling and makes it easier to recover lost or stolen cattle.

Today ranchers often use electric branding irons, but when we were kids, it was done the old-fashioned way. During roundup we had a fire burning all day and kept the business end of the branding iron in the fire. When it was red-hot, it was pressed briefly into the side or hip of the calf and, in a puff of foul-smelling blue smoke, the calf was branded.

The brand for the Nelson Ranch was the "quarter-circle-N-bar" brand. It consisted of an "N" with a quarter circle above it and a bar (line) under it. Brands are read top to bottom and left to right.

BLUE SMOKE RISES DURING BRANDING.

When cattle are branded, they usually have their ears marked as a supplemental form of identification. The ear markings for the Nelson Ranch were a crop (tip removed) in the right ear and a split in the left. In addition an ear tag with a number on it was usually applied to the calf. The brand and ear markings identified it as a Nelson calf, but the ear tag number identified which specific one. An ear tag was used to track a particular calf throughout its life on the ranch. We didn't name our cattle, but ranch records tracked every one by ear tag number. The records might show that #432 is a heifer that was born in spring of 1979 and sold in fall of 1982. The hired hand might tell Dad that #325 looks like she's ready to calve any day now, but #251 looks sick.

Another thing we did with calves at roundup was to de-horn them. This was done by cutting off the nubbin horn and searing the nub with a hot iron. We didn't want the cattle to have horns because they could be hazardous to people as well as other cattle. Many ranchers seek bulls without the

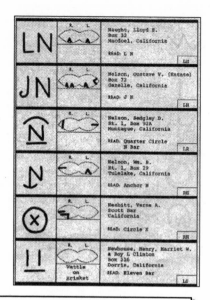

ABOVE LEFT: COVER OF THE 1960 BOOK OF LIVESTOCK BRANDS FOR SISKIYOU COUNTY.

ABOVE RIGHT: PAGE 97 OF THE 1960 LIVESTOCK BRANDS BOOK SHOWS THE NELSON RANCH "QUARTER CIRCLE N BAR" BRAND (THIRD FROM TOP). TO THE RIGHT OF THE BRAND IS A DIAGRAM SHOWING THE EAR MARKINGS FOR THE NELSON CATTLE: CROP IN RIGHT AND SPLIT IN LEFT. THE "LR" INDICATES THE LOCATION (LEFT RIB) WHERE THE BRAND IS APPLIED.

genetic "recipe" for horns to avoid the problems that come with horned cattle.

Roundup was also the time when we castrated the male calves. A steer is a castrated bull, and steers make better meat and are easier to raise, so most herds consist primarily of heifers and steers. The rare male calf may be spared so it can become a breeder bull, but normally a new bull is acquired from outside the herd to ensure genetic diversity and to preclude the manifestation of genetic defects. In the early years, castration was done with a sharp knife, but in later years it was done with a strong rubber band that was clamped around the testicles. The rubber band cut off the blood supply, and nature eventually took its course. The rubber band technique also lessened the chance of infection. Most ranchers tend to sleep with their legs crossed for a few weeks after roundup.

Roundup was a dusty, dirty, sweaty, bloody, smelly event, but it had its rituals and eating mountain oysters was one of them. Calf testicles are called *fries* in the meat market, but the colloquial term for them is *mountain oysters*. Part of establishing manhood and being a "real rancher" was eating mountain oysters during roundup. We always had a branding fire going and a pot of hot coffee that was so strong we could float a pistol in it. In addition we would sometimes cook a cake on top of the fire and fry mountain oysters, which were plentiful before the day was over.

I was just a kid, but I drank the coffee, ate the cake and tasted the mountain oysters so I could be a "real man." Been there, done that, don't have to do it again.

CHAPTER TEN

THE SPACE RACE COMES TO THE RANCH

Growing up on the ranch in the 1950s, my brothers and I were greatly influenced by the Space Age that began in 1957, also called the "space race." It wasn't until we were much older that we learned that the space race was part of the rivalry between the United States and the former Soviet Union called the Cold War. Man had not yet reached Earth orbit or the moon, but our scientists were building bigger rockets and testing the limits of man's endurance with rocket sleds and centrifuges.

The burning question among scientists in the 1950s was whether the human body could endure the rigors of space travel. We didn't have television on the ranch yet, but when we went to the movies, we saw newsreels and sat in awe as they showed men spun senseless in giant centrifuges and alternately flattened into their seats, blasted forward bug-eyed, then slammed to a stop in rocket sleds. For us, the space race was high-tech science and exciting stuff.

Inspired by these brave astronauts engaged in a venture that we all expected would one day take men to outer space, my bother Tom and I began to think about how we could contribute to the effort. Reflecting on the newsreels we had seen, we decided that our efforts should, at least initially, be focused on testing the limits of man's endurance to physical stress. Our early experiments were somewhat primitive and made little use of technology. We would spin in circles until we were too dizzy to stand then fall against Mom's favorite lamp. From these experiments we learned that there were limits to the number of rotations we could make without throwing up, and that there were also limits to what Mom would let us do in the house. Science advances by learning from its mistakes.

Moving outside, we continued to experiment with spinning trials. Tom, as the oldest and biggest brother, would grab my wrists and yank me off my feet, spinning me in wide circles. Tom found this more fun than I did, and I can still recall his laughter as, breathlessly, I would form the words, "Stop! I'm going to throw up." Tom interpreted this plea to mean that he should spin me harder and faster. Despite these communications glitches and contrary to my hypothesis, we found that I couldn't throw up when being spun by the wrists. On the other hand, when spun by the feet, it was easy. I sometimes suspected that certain experiments were designed more for Tom's entertainment at my expense than as true scientific endeavors.

I always assumed that the human glider experiments he invented fell into this category. In the human glider test flights, Tom would grab one of my wrists and one of my ankles and spin me around in great loops, undulating from ground-skimming lows to breathtaking highs. This, however, was not the human glider experiment itself. This was just the warm up. The human glider experiment was initiated when Tom would let go at the point of maximum spin and maximum height.

Discounting the rather short-term effects of inertia, we repeatedly demonstrated that the glide ratio of the human body is approximately 0 to 1. Put another way, I invariably fell immediately from whatever height I had reached when Tom let go, without exhibiting any detectable tendency to glide. Further experimentation demonstrated that donning a cape, such as Superman was known to wear, did not noticeably improve my glide ratio. I remember that this last finding was particularly disappointing. Just to be sure, we experimented with a variety of capes. While old curtains were found to make better capes than dishtowels, neither enhanced my glide ratio to a measurable degree.

Turning from these low-tech experiments in which I was the human guinea pig, we began to conceive high-tech experiments with animals. It had not escaped our notice that other scientists often used animals as test subjects. We did not have guinea pigs or monkeys at our disposal on the ranch, but there was always an abundance of cats around the place. With cat in hand, we turned to the only obvious and available high-tech device available to simulate the centrifuge experiments we had seen on the newsreels.

Scientists used these experiments to determine whether man could tolerate the discomfort and function while experiencing the G forces they would endure as they were shot into space. These same conditions, we surmised, could be duplicated with Mom's washing machine on the spin dry cycle. We considered these experiments very dangerous and always appointed a safety officer. If we ever got caught, we could have been spanked. Therefore, we were forced to conduct these experiments in Mom's absence. She did not seem share our interest in scientific experimentation anyway. It was the safety officer's job to make sure Mom wasn't anywhere near when experimentation was under way, a mission deemed more critical than ensuring the safety of the participants.

Our experiments with cats on spin dry were somewhat inconclusive. Having endured the spin dry cycle, a cat would be disoriented for a brief period but would then rapidly depart from the testing grounds before the total effects could be assessed. We did note, however, that the experience would cause the cat to relieve itself in the washing machine. I remember Mom would remark how the washing machine smelled funny sometimes. Tom and I would shrug our shoulders, flash our most practiced looks of childlike innocence and get lost as rapidly as possible.

The washing machine experiments demonstrated to our satisfaction that humans, or at least cats, could survive the G forces associated with being shot into space. However, there remained the nagging question as to whether man, or animal, could function or perform critical maneuvers while experiencing these G forces. To solve this question we again took cat in hand and turned to another household wonder of technology, the clothes dryer.

This experiment required two people, a cat and the assurance that Mom was distracted. We discovered that when the dryer was turned on, it would not rotate until the little button in the door latch was depressed by closing the door. When we stuffed the cat into the dryer and closed the door, we could hear that things were happening inside, but we could not observe exactly how well the cat was performing in this particular experiment. Our ingenious solution was to leave the dryer door open and to press the activation button by hand. This worked fine, and we found that cats perform exceptionally well under such adverse conditions.

All our feline test pilots, we further concluded, had a strong preference for not remaining in the dryer when it was in motion. In spite of the rotation, the cat was able to leap from the dryer whenever it found solid footing which, as it turned out, was about every other rotation. With the cat playing the role of a reluctant astronaut, my job was to catch the cat when it jumped out and return it to the dryer so the experiment could continue. This was a two-handed job, and gloves were advisable. With both of my hands occupied, Tom's job was to hold the dryer door open with one hand and push the button to activate the dryer with the other, while looking over his shoulder to see if Mom was coming.

These experiments convinced us that man, or cat, should be able to function reasonably well under the adverse conditions associated with space travel. However, the question that continued to burn in our minds was this: How could we safely bring man, or cat, back to earth once in space? A parachute seemed the logical answer to the reentry challenge.

We developed our own parachute technology through systematic experimentation. A handkerchief, some string and a plastic soldier made an excellent prototype. We developed ever-improved parachutes by varying the length of the strings, adding weights and finding new ways to fold the chute so that we could throw it high in the air without having it open too soon or too late, and without the strings becoming entangled. Once we had honed our parachute technology to a fine edge, it was time for the big experiment.

As usual, we were not able to enlist a volunteer from among the ranks of the ranch's feline residents. It seems that over time, the cats had developed a propensity to split whenever one of us kids appeared. Finally, after much consideration, the slowest of the litter was selected for the experiment. Clearly a handkerchief would not be adequate for this reentry experiment. It was too small relative to the size and weight of the cat. We selected the finest of Mom's tea towels from the kitchen. We carefully measured and cut strong strings and rigged a harness. The cat was fit into the harness, and the parachute carefully folded for action. We were ready!

In retrospect, I should have been able to predict the failure of this particular experiment. Trying to launch a cat with your bare hands was asking for trouble. I should have anticipated that cats wouldn't like to be launched into space, and I should have remembered a key finding from our clothes dryer research, the value of wearing gloves. Further, to my regret, I didn't yet realize that a cat's every instinct is to remain earthbound and that it has a natural reflex action that causes it to grasp and cling to any delivery system that would attempt to launch it into space.

As we prepared for liftoff, I checked all systems, retracted my arm, activated forward thrust and as my hand reached maximum launch velocity, I released the cat. But the cat didn't release me. It had engaged its braking system, which employed 10 pointy things on the ends of its toes. In a flash of pain and the mutual screams of cat and boy, the cat was airborne. My enduring souvenir of this particular scientific experiment was 10 cat claw marks starting at my wrist and extending to the tips of my fingers.

Cats are quick and vengeful, but not particularly well versed in the dynamics of parachuting. Once airborne, the cat, being somewhat anxious, grasped at anything in its vicinity. Unfortunately, the only thing in its vicinity in mid air was the parachute. There is a long-standing principle in parachuting that says, essentially, a grasped parachute doesn't open. And it didn't. Fortunately, the cat wasn't injured, but I acquired painful and long-lasting scars to remind me of the design flaws in this particular exercise. In the end, the only scientific information we came up with was confirmation that a cat lands on its feet when it drops from just about any height.

Tom and I were inspired by the concept of space travel and marveled at the technology and bravery of would-be astronauts. This sense of wonder stimulated our experimentation but, in the end, we failed to make any significant contributions to the space race. I attribute this more to our lack of funding than to a deficiency in imagination or effort. Despite the lack of overall success in our Nelson Ranch space program, I may – as a result of the re-entry experiment – qualify as one of the first casualties in the space race.

I should emphasize that our parents were unaware of our participation in the space race and associated experimentation; it was top-secret at the time. With the passing of both parents, I feel I can safely release the above declassified account of our involvement. I would also like to offer my apologies to the brave, if reluctant, feline astronauts. They demonstrated repeatedly that ranch cats are made of the "right stuff." Thankfully, none of the astro-cats perished or received lasting injuries as a result of their contributions to science. The scratches I incurred exceeded any physical damage the cats may have suffered, and rightfully so.

CHAPTER ELEVEN

IRRIGATING

Boiled down to its essence, a rancher's job is to make big cows out of little cows and sell them for a profit. This takes grass, and grass takes water. That's why, in high-desert country, one of the most meaningful measures of a valuable cattle ranch is the amount of irrigated pastureland it contains.

CURIOUS CATTLE IN FIELD NO. 4 LOOK ON AS THEIR PICTURE IS TAKEN.

Irrigation is the process of delivering water from a water supply, through a delivery system of pumps, pipes, dams and ditches to a pasture.

Wild grasses grow on the open range, but in Siskiyou County, the wild grasses generally dry up after the rainy season has run its course from October to June. Once the cattle eat down the range grass, it won't grow back until the next rainy season.

The advantage of irrigated pasture is that it receives water throughout the growing season and produces a reliable source of feed for the cattle. The grasses grown in irrigated pastures are usually much more nutritious than dry range grass. The cattle may eat the grass down in an irrigated field, but, when the cattle are rotated into another field, it quickly grows back. Without irrigated pasture, a ranch would need many thousands of acres of range grass to support a modest herd of cattle.

As a rule of thumb, the more irrigated pasture you have, the more cattle you can raise; and the more cattle you raise, the greater chance you have of actually making a profit, which is why you bought a ranch in the first place. Nutritious feed grown in an irrigated pasture helps the cattle put on weight fast. This is a good thing because when you sell them, you will be paid by the pound. This should make sense because when you buy a steak in the supermarket, you pay a higher price for a big steak than you do for a little steak. The rancher's goal is to sell big steaks rather than little steaks – on the hoof.

The Nelson Ranch had more than 200 acres of irrigated pasture and from 200 to 450 cattle, depending on the year or time of year. For a time we used some of the irrigated pasture to grow alfalfa for hay to feed the cattle through the winter. Eventually my father decided it was better to convert the alfalfa field into pastureland, so he could expand his herd. He figured it made more sense to have a larger herd and to buy his winter hay from someone else.

WATER SUPPLY AND WATER RIGHTS

Agriculture of any kind requires water. Whether you have a garden at your home in the city, or own a fig orchard or a cattle ranch in the country, you need water for irrigation in order to grow crops or critters. In the city, if you lose your irrigation water supply, you lose your garden. But you can still buy your vegetables at the supermarket. In the country, if you lose your irrigation water supply, you lose your livelihood and you won't have money to buy food at the supermarket. Water is especially important for farmers and ranchers, but it's important to everybody because everybody likes to eat. The food you buy in the supermarket depends on someone, somewhere having a water supply.

Since water is a limited resource and everybody depends on it, individuals, states and even nations have battled over access to water and water rights throughout history. Everybody needs water to live, and many need it to make a living. Water is also an important environmental issue because trees, plants and wildlife depend on natural water supplies.

Today the issue of agricultural water rights and water access is extremely complicated and controversial because ranchers, farmers, attorneys, property owners, environmentalists, governmental regulators and politicians all have interests in water and water rights. Each party in a water-rights dispute champions his or her own rights, needs or wishes; and it is difficult, if not impossible, to find a way for everybody to win. Ongoing battles over water generate much heat and smoke, but it doesn't appear that there will ever be enough water to cool the dispute.

Most of the Nelson Ranch's water supply for irrigation came from the Shasta River. The river marked the southern and western boundaries of the ranch, and the legal right to the water came with the ranch. A pump on the river near the southern property line pulled water from the river and delivered it to a ditch that ran for well over a mile and irrigated five separate pastures. We added three more pastures later, but their water came from a well we dug near the ranch house. The well couldn't provide as much water as the river did, and the water was not as good for irrigating. It had a high mineral content, and some of the minerals were less than optimal for plant health.

PUMPS, HEAD GATES, OUTLETS, CHECKS AND SETS

There are many ways to deliver water for irrigation. The best choice depends on the type of crop or herd you are growing, the nature of the water supply and how much money you have to spend. Some operations use sprinklers or drip systems, but the least expensive and most common way to irrigate is by flooding. With flood irrigation, water is released from a pipe or ditch and allowed to flow into the area being irrigated. The Nelson Ranch used flood irrigation for all eight pastures.

Irrigation is not rocket science, but it does involve a certain amount of technology and includes its own terminology. The ranch irrigation system was low-tech, but it worked reasonably well. The system's heart was a pump that pulled the water from the river, pushed it some 200 feet up a hill through a 10-inch diameter pipe and dumped it into the irrigation ditch.

The pump was housed in a cinderblock pump house my father built shortly after we moved onto the ranch in 1947. The pump ran on electricity and made a lot of noise. The pump house was a dark, dank, loud place; and, as a kid, I always felt it was a scary place. I didn't like loud mechanical noises, so I avoided going into the pump house as much as possible.

The pump pulled water from the Shasta River through an uptake pipe that extended into a trench that connected with the river about 8 feet away. The river water flowed into the trench, which served as a sort of collection reservoir. When I was a kid, my father frequently warned me not to go near the edge of the trench. The loud pump, the dark swirling water and the steep edges of the trench made it creepy and dangerous. For years I imagined how horrible it would be to fall into that dark swirling reservoir and get sucked into the pump.

In order to keep turtles, frogs, moss, little kids and other river flotsam and jetsam from being sucked into the pump, Dad installed a half-inch mesh screen system in the trench between the uptake pipe and the river. Despite Dad's efforts, moss, sticks, turtles and other debris would occasionally bypass the screen system, get sucked into the pump and lodge themselves there.

When debris got past the screen system and was sucked into the pump, it would often clog the pump and greatly reduce its efficiency. Water-flow would diminish accordingly. When this happened, there wouldn't be enough water to irrigate efficiently, so we would have to shut the pump off, take it apart and clean out the debris to get things back into working order.

Turtles were abundant along the river and mobile enough to get past the screen system with some regularity. For their troubles, they were sucked into the pump, where they were immediately shredded by the spinning impeller. In order to remove the larger turtle parts that became lodged in the pump, we had to shut the pump off and turn a large wheel that closed a gate valve in the pipe. This kept water in the pipe above the pump so it would be available to re-prime the pump when we started it again.

Next we had to unbolt and remove the heavy, cast metal, top housing of the pump assembly. This revealed the pump impeller that sat in a reservoir of water in the lower half of the pump assembly. After making doubly sure the power was turned off, we would remove by hand any obvious debris that was clogged in the impeller.

Next came the fun part. We had to roll up our sleeves and reach deep into the dark reservoir beneath the impeller.

Down there we would feel around until we found all of the turtle parts that were wedged here and there. Sometimes we found pieces of snakes and frogs too. After all critter parts were removed, we put everything back together and restarted the pump. Cleaning out the pump was one thing during the day when there was light coming through the window. It was quite another thing when you had to do it in the middle of the night with no illumination other than a flashlight.

After the pump appeared to be running properly, we walked up the hill to where the pipe poured water into the ditch to make sure the proper water flow had been restored. The sound of the pump and the level of water in the pipe were our assurance everything was working properly. When the pump was partially blocked or not running efficiently, it made a rattling sound that could be heard above its usual racket. When the pump was working properly, the noise was loud and smooth. If there was no more than a 3-inch gap between the surface of the water in the pipe and the top of the pipe, the water flow was good and everything was working well.

IRRIGATION WATER
FLOWS FROM A "SET"
THROUGH AN "OUTLET"
TO FLOOD A "CHECK."

When the pump was putting sufficient water into the ditch, we were ready to irrigate. It would have taken a huge ditch and a torrent of water to irrigate all of the fields at once. With our more modest system, we could only irrigate one small field or a section of a large field at a time. To irrigate a section of pasture, we had to dam or block the flow of water in the ditch so that the water would back up and flow out of "outlets" that were dug into the pasture side of the ditch. Each outlet allowed water to flood a section of the pasture that was usually bounded by subtle ridges. We called the section of pasture irrigated by a single outlet a "check." The ditch carried enough water to irrigate around 20 checks from 20 outlets at a time, when the ditch was dammed. The section of ditch that was dammed in order to irrigate a specific section of pasture was called a "set."

WATER FLOWING THROUGH AN OPEN "HEAD GATE."

When we moved onto the ranch, we "made a set" by placing a canvas dam in the ditch. Irrigating in those days usually meant getting wet because the person placing the canvas dam had to get into the water. The canvas dam consisted of a large piece of canvas attached to a long wooden pole. When not in use, the canvas was rolled around the pole so you could carry it to the next set. When deployed as a dam, the pole was placed across the ditch and the canvas was unfurled and dropped into the ditch. Rocks were placed around the edges to hold the canvas down and seal it against the bottom and sides of the ditch. When the flow was blocked, the water backed up and began to flow out of the outlets to irrigate the checks that were part of that particular set.

Not too many years after we moved onto the ranch, my father began installing fixed dams in the ditch at the locations where the canvas dams were usually deployed to make a set. The fixed dams consisted of a cement wall across the ditch with a large hole in the middle of it. Normally the water flowed through the hole, but if you wanted to block the flow to make a set, a large, flat piece of sheet metal was lowered across the front of the hole. This blocked the water from running through and turned the wall into a dam. The sheet metal cover was usually raised and lowered by cables attached to a crank mounted on a metal frame embedded in the cement wall.

These "high tech" ditch dams were called "head gates." You cranked the metal plate up to let the water flow, and you lowered it down to make a dam so you could irrigate the set behind it. Not a complicated system, but much more efficient and easier to work with than the portable canvas dams.

There were about 30 sets in the five fields irrigated by the river pump. Depending on the size of the set and slope of the field, it took from 4 to 12 hours to flood a set, with the average time being around 8 to 10 hours. A set was considered properly irrigated when the water from every outlet in the set flooded its corresponding check from the ditch to the lowest part of the pasture below it. It took 12 to 15 days to irrigate all five fields. By then it was usually time to start the cycle all over again. If we had a good rain or the weather was cool, we could sometimes shut the pump off for a couple of days. But it ran most of the time during the normal April-to-September irrigation season.

DOING THE IRRIGATING

One of the dubious privileges of growing up on a ranch is that at some point about age 12, you're old enough to "do the irrigating." At one time or another, both Tom and I were assigned the job for the summer. As low-tech as irrigating was, there were still ways for a kid to screw it up, and I developed a certain expertise in finding them. Dad was a highly organized, systematized, methodical worker. As a kid, I was none of these. On top of this, I had a bad attitude. I considered irrigation chores as something like slave labor. I saw myself as an unwilling conscript who was responsible for doing the irrigating, and Dad was the "irrigation police."

Every day when Dad got home from work he gave me a harrowing cross-examination about how the work was going. An "irrigation interrogation" might go something like this:

Dad would start by asking, "Where's the water?"

I would answer, "Uh...it's in the second set in No. 3 Field."

"What time did you change the water?"

"Uh.....about 1:30...I think."

"You didn't look at the clock? That set takes about 10 hours. If you changed it at 1:30, you'll have to check it at 11:30 tonight."

"Yes."

"Yes, what?!"

"Yes sir, it was 1:30, and I'll check it at 11:30 tonight."

"Did you have a full head of water?"

"Well, it seemed to be going OK."

"Did you check the pump and clean the screen?"

"I was planning to do that in the morning."

"You'll do it tonight when you check the water."

"OK." (*Aw nuts, now I'll have to go down to the pump after dark.*)

"Did you walk the checks to see if the first set in No. 3 was done before you changed the water?"

"Most of it."

"You didn't check it all?"

"Not quite."

"How did you know it was time to change the water if you didn't walk the checks?"

"It seemed like it was done...I thought it was done."

"You'd better hope it was done."

"I'm pretty sure."

"Did you spend any time cutting down the milkweed in No. 4?"

"Not today."

"How about the bull thistles?"

"Not today."

"Well what the 'H' did you do today besides change the water?"

"Uh....Larry Jones came over, and we went fishing."

"You're gonna work on those milkweeds and thistles tomorrow."

"That's just what I was thinking."

It cost money to run the pump to irrigate the fields. During the hot summer, you had to keep the water moving as fast as possible so all the fields would be irrigated before they started to dry out. If you changed a set too soon, before the water had saturated that section of pasture, it would leave a dry spot that turned an ugly brown. Dad could spot a brown spot in a green field from the next county. "You missed a spot in No. 1," he'd say. "Are you walking those checks before you change the water?"

"I must have missed a spot."

"You sure as 'H' did."

"I'll be sure to get it next time."

"You sure as 'H' will."

MOSQUITOES, SNAKES, GOPHERS AND WEREWOLVES

Now that you have a basic understanding of the process, I'll take you out with me so you can see irrigating through the eyes of a kid. It's 9:45 p.m. on a warm summer night. It's quite dark outside, but you have been reminded to go "check the water."

Step No. 1 is to slather up with mosquito repellent. The only stuff around in those days was something called "6-12," and it was oily, smelled really bad, tasted horrible if it got in your mouth and stung like a banshee when it got in your eyes. At some point on each occasion when you anointed yourself with 6-12, you'd manage to get some in your mouth and your eyes. It was all a necessary part of the ritual of irrigating.

Step No. 2: find the flashlight and a shovel. The flashlights we used were the kind we called miner lights. They had a battery pack that clipped on your belt or went into your back pocket. The light bulb itself was connected to the battery pack with a long cable. An elastic strap held the light to your hat or around your forehead so the light would shine in the direction you were looking. This kept your hands free to work.

Since it's getting even darker fast, the next step is trying to con one of your brothers into going with you. Everybody knows that monsters only attack you when you are alone. If you have one other person with you, even a little brother, you will be safe. Unfortunately, it was a rare night indeed when I could persuade someone to go with me into the black abyss that began at the back door. This makes it imperative to get a good old ranch dog to go with you. Dogs don't keep monsters away, but they just might delay the monster long enough so you can escape its clutches. Anyway, the dog will give you a companion to talk to when you are nervous about being out there in the dark. It's pretty easy to get a dog to go with you. They are almost always eager to go anywhere you're going. Just start the pickup, and they show up ready to go.

Now that you are slathered with 6-12, and have your dog, shovel and flashlight, you're ready to go irrigating. Soon you're bouncing along a dusty, bumpy ranch road in the pickup. Your headlights chase away a small patch of darkness in front of you, but beyond that there's an inky blackness. It's "country dark," that is, there are no streetlights, no visible city or house lights, just darkness and any faint glow you might get from the moon and the stars.

You could kick yourself for asking Mom to take you to the movie "I Was a Teenage Werewolf" a few nights before. The last thing you need as you head into the night is visions of werewolves. You realize they probably don't exist, but if they do, they certainly hang out in the country, and one can never be too sure about such things. It's just your bad luck to have to change the water in the middle of the night after seeing that movie. While wondering if 6-12 repels werewolves, you vow to be extra alert on this trip.

By the time ranch kids are 10 years old, they are experienced ranch drivers. As soon as you can see over the dashboard and reach the important pedals, you are ready to start driving on the ranch. You don't drive off the property or on any paved roads; but you know what most of the knobs and pedals do, and you can steer around most of the big rocks and holes well enough for ranch driving.

The noise of the motor and the pickup's headlights are comforting as you drive away from the ranch house and the last vestiges of civilization. You are like a moving island of light in the midst of a sea of blackness. Sagebrush and juniper trees cast suspicious drifting shadows as your headlights move across them. There's nothing friendly out there. You are on your own, and your only friends are your flashlight, the shovel (which could be used as a weapon if necessary) and the dog. But, come to think of it, you haven't seen the dog in quite a while. It could be chasing something, or it could be that something out there snatched it.

You stop in front of a closed gate. When you get out of the truck to open it, everything is OK because your headlights shine upon the scene. It's another story after you drive through the gate and go back to close it behind you. Your headlights are pointed away, and you are in almost utter darkness. The only light you have is the dim red glow from the taillights of the pickup. You struggle frantically with the gate to get it closed before something evil moves in on you. In your haste, you cut yourself on the barbed wire and pinch yourself in the gate, a small price to pay for such risky business.

Finally you arrive at the location where you are to "check the water." You position the pickup as close to where you will be working as possible. A quick dash from the field and you'd reach safety. Before you turn off the engine and headlights, you turn on the flashlight. You kill the engine and headlights, and let the quiet darkness close in around you. The only sounds are your footsteps, crickets and the occasional frog. If you are in luck, the coyotes aren't howling tonight. You know that coyotes are just dogs, but a coyote howl in the darkness of night has a lonesome, eerie sound that makes your blood run cold. Of course there's the possibility that werewolves wail just like coyotes. How would you know the difference? It's always better to hear coyotes howling when there are a lot of other people around.

A dim flashlight is a pathetic glow against the miles of blackness that stretch out in every direction around you, but it's all you have. You need a good light to spot real hazards like snakes as well as the imaginary hazards like the monsters of whatever sort that might be out there. Since the ranch is rattlesnake country, you learn to always be on the lookout when you're walking around. A few close calls with rattlesnakes will sharpen your senses. In time, your snake-awareness faculties are so finely tuned that you tend to walk around in a state that is something like a coiled spring trap. The slightest movement or slither at your feet sends you instantly skyward. As often as not, the slither comes from a harmless water snake or gopher snake, a blue-belly lizard or a mouse, but you can make that determination after you come down several feet away from where you had the encounter.

Once you calm down, your first irrigating task is to make sure that the current set is completely flooded. To do this you must walk into the field and go to the downhill end of the section of pasture. You walk along each check, stomping your feet to make sure the water has reached this far. If all has gone well, the set is done and you can change the water to the next set. If all is not going well, then you can figure that a turtle is caught in the pump, and you'll have to go down to the pump house in the middle of the night, take it apart, remove the turtle parts, put the pump back together, start it and wait for the water to reach the portion of ditch where you're supposed to be irrigating.

Tonight, you are in luck. The set is completely flooded, and you can move the water to the next set. You begin this process by hiking along the ditch to the end of the next set to make sure the head gate is closed and the ditch is dammed. Then you open the head gate for the current set and let the water rush through into the next set. It normally takes about 20 minutes for the water to reach the closed head gate and back up enough to start flowing out of the outlets. Now you have to inspect every outlet in the new set to make sure that they are all working properly. You use your shovel to open outlets that are flowing too slowly and to narrow outlets that are running too fast.

Finally, you have to walk the ditch along the previous set to make sure that none of the outlets are still flowing. This is where you will need the shovel again. If you don't close up all the outlets after you have finished with a set, your water supply will bleed off, and you will not have enough water flow to properly irrigate the next set. Since the water level in each set drops after you open the head gate, it's usually not much of a chore to make sure none of the outlets in the previously irrigated set are still running. Sometimes the outlets will be closed, but you may still find water flowing from the ditch through a gopher hole in the ditch bank. These gopher holes must be closed up to keep the irrigation water level up to snuff.

Gophers and ditches are a bad combination, so any time a gopher makes the mistake of coming out of its hole when you're irrigating, you will be sure to kill it. A good whack with the shovel does the trick, but care must be exercised because, chances are, the dog has spotted the gopher too and is going for it at the same time. More than one ranch dog fell victim to "friendly fire" and was unintentionally shovel-whacked when I was trying to dispatch a gopher.

This all takes time, and the process takes even longer because, from time to time it is necessary to stop and stand perfectly still so you can just listen. If you stop suddenly in your tracks but still hear footsteps behind you in the darkness, it's probably a werewolf – just like in the movie. You can't be too careful or too prepared for such things, so you occasionally take a few practice swings with the shovel. This, you figure, would impress and be an obvious warning to any monsters or werewolves loitering in the vicinity; but it also scares the piss out of the dog, which is your only ally out there. After a shovel-swinging outburst, it's usually necessary to reassure the dog that you mean him no harm and you really are his very best friend.

As you hurry along, you are generally oblivious to the ubiquitous mosquitoes that are so very glad to see you out there in the night. Mosquitoes hone in on your light and the carbon dioxide you exhale. They feast on your blood, right through the repellent, which they seem to regard as something like steak sauce. Given the possibility of an imminent encounter with a werewolf, mosquitoes are the least of your concerns. You swat your way through the horde and continue your chores.

In your haste to finish, you soon find that you are breathing hard; irrigating at warp-speed is not a chore for sissies. Working hard and fast is good exercise, but the downside of getting winded while irrigating is that it increases the chances that you will inhale a mosquito. If you haven't snorted a mosquito up your nose, you can't appreciate the experience. Apparently a snorted mosquito ends up soaked with saliva and clinging with all six legs to the backside of your uvula. Here it can withstand hurricane-force winds and floods of saliva as its host repeatedly probes, snorts, coughs, gags and engages in loud throat-clearing exercises in a futile effort to dislodge the little sucker. I think the typical inhaled mosquito manages to hang on until it, or its host, dies a natural death. If the mosquito dies first, it can be dislodged and swallowed, or spit out at the host's option.

Work fast, try to dislodge the mosquito in your windpipe, stop, listen, swing the shovel, call the dog, pet and reassure the dog, and keep working. Before you know it, you are done. The water is changed – now all you have to do is get back to the house before something attacks you, and you die a horrible death in the darkness in the middle of nowhere.

You push the pickup to its maximum potential and set land-speed records on the way back to the safety of the house at the conclusion of an after-dark irrigation session. You roar into the yard and lock up the brakes, causing the pickup to skid sideways in the gravel before coming to a stop. Before the trailing plume of dust settles, you are striding through the back door and into the blessed light.

Your heart is still racing, but you are as cool as a cucumber when Mom asks, "How'd it go?"

"No problems," you reply nonchalantly, realizing there's no point in giving a fuller account of the perils you survived. How could a mere mortal possibly appreciate your bravery in the face of such close encounters with snakes, monsters and werewolves in the night? You are a ranch kid, and ranch kids do the irrigation, day and night, regardless of the hazards awaiting you at the end of an irrigation ditch, just beyond the end of a dirt road.

CHAPTER TWELVE

SCHOOL DAYS

One of the minor disadvantages of growing up on a ranch was its isolation. Most of the time there was nobody to play with except my brothers. Brothers are OK when there is nobody else, but, as anybody who has ever lived with siblings knows, age differences define an intellectual and physical pecking order that complicates things. As a general rule, big brothers don't want to play with little brothers, but little brothers always want to play with big brothers.

This interplay of isolation, age differences and normal sibling competition set the stage for conflicts, arguments, fights and rivalries that persisted at least until high school. I was closest in age to my brother Tom, but he was two years older and much larger physically than I was. David was five years younger than I was, and Dan was another five years younger than David. Age gaps of two, five or 10 years mean nothing to adults, but among kids these gaps represent almost insurmountable differences in interests, abilities, size and maturity.

David probably had the worst of it because he was in the middle with nobody within five years of his age to play with and only one younger brother to pick on. Dan was the youngest, and while he didn't have any younger brothers to harass, he had three older ones to follow around and pester. As is typical with most families, Dan also enjoyed the benefits that come with being the "baby of the family." He got away with things and enjoyed privileges that none of us older siblings could or would have dreamed of. In Dan's case, one of the downsides of being the youngest was that he was still in his teens and living at home when our parents went through their divorce. That's an experience one doesn't want to be close to at any age.

While Tom was away at school, I had 1,704 acres to play on but nobody to play with since David and Dan hadn't been born yet. It was a bit lonely at the end of a dirt road with no daytime companions, so I eagerly looked forward to the day when I could go to school with the big kids.

CEREAL BOX WARS

It was an exciting day when I was finally old enough to join my big brother Tom when he left for school. School days began with a breakfast that usually consisted of cereal, or what we called "mush." The mush was either oatmeal or Cream of Wheat. If we had cereal, it would usually be Cheerios, Wheaties, Quaker Puffed Wheat or Rice, Shredded Wheat or Rice Crispies. We liked Cheerios because it was advertised on the "Lone Ranger" radio program. We liked Wheaties because it was advertised as the "breakfast of champions" or, as we called it, the "breakfast of chimpanzees." Quaker Puffed Wheat was good because it was advertised on the "Sergeant Preston" (of the Yukon) radio show as the only cereal "shot from guns." Shredded Wheat was good because the cardboard dividers that separated the layers of biscuits in the box had handy tips on camping and outdoor life. These tips were attributed to an (American) Indian whose name I have forgotten, but it was something like Straight Arrow. Straight Arrow's tips explained how to build a raft from logs, a tepee with poles and a blanket, or a bridge over a creek – all handy stuff for ranch kids.

When we had cereal for breakfast, the standard procedure was to appropriate as many cereal boxes as we could. We arranged them in front of us on the table to form a privacy wall. This way you could hunker down in your "fort" behind the cereal boxes and look at the pictures on the boxes while eating like a pig without having to look at your brothers and without attracting parental attention. It was important to lay claim to the best cereal boxes as soon as you sat down; otherwise your brothers would grab the best ones, and you would have to eat out in the open. There were many arguments over who was entitled to which cereal boxes during breakfast.

On weekends or special occasions, Mom made fried or scrambled eggs and bacon for breakfast. We particularly liked "popovers," which were cooked in a cupcake pan. The popovers looked like a bread cupcake that leaned to one side. They were eaten with syrup or jam. Corn fritters were another favorite. Embedded with kernels of corn, the deep-fried fritters were dipped in maple syrup before we gobbled them down. Waffles and pancakes were other breakfast favorites. On most school days, however, breakfast usually consisted of cereal or mush with toast, sometimes with raisins for variation.

BIG SPRINGS ELEMENTARY SCHOOL

The ranch was located in the Big Springs School District. The school didn't have a kindergarten so we started school in the first grade. Our mother or father would drive us the dusty or muddy mile to where Nelson Road connected with the paved county road. A small yellow bus picked us up by the mailbox and hauled us the three or so miles to the Big Springs School. Sometimes my father drove us all the way to school on his way to work. At the end of the school day, the bus dropped us off at the mailbox, and Mom picked us up or we walked the mile to the house.

In 1948 when Tom was in the first grade, he had to walk the mile from the mailbox to the house in a blizzard. A severe snowstorm hit the county, and school was let out early so the children could get home before everyone was snowed in. My mother was home, but since we had no phone, she had no idea that school was ending early. The bus dropped Tom off at the mailbox, and he walked the mile to the house in the "Blizzard of '48," the worst storm to hit the county in all the years we lived there. I'd like to think a school wouldn't send a first grader into a blizzard today.

The Big Springs schoolhouse was a classic building made of red brick with a bell tower in the front. It was staffed by two teachers and housed eight grades in two classrooms. Grades 1 through 4 met in one room and Grades 5 through 8 in the other. Boys' and girls' bathrooms were located at opposite ends of a common hallway that was called the "cloakroom" and was lined with hooks on which we hung our jackets and rain gear. During the wet and muddy winter months, we often wore large waterproof overshoes which slipped over our regular shoes and were cinched shut with a series of metal clasps. Our parents called them "galoshes," but the teacher called them "rubbers," and we were instructed to leave them in the cloakroom.

A large bell in the bell tower at the front of the school was rung to announce the start of school or the end of recess or lunch break. A teacher usually rang the bell, but sometimes a student was allowed to do so. It was somewhat of an honor to ring the bell, so I eagerly waited for the opportunity. When I was finally granted the privilege, I found I was too short to reach the rope that hung from the bell. Big John, a large 8th grader, lifted me so I could reach the rope, but

I found I was too light to move the heavy bell at the top of the tower. I just dangled from the rope with my feet off the floor. Finally Big John took the rope and rang the bell for me while I bobbed up and down on end of the rope. One of the teachers standing nearby sternly told me that little kids shouldn't try to ring the bell.

Sometimes a hand-held bell would be rung to announce the end of recess. When the bell clanged from the steps of the schoolhouse, kids would come running from all corners of the playground. Smaller kids could wield the hand-held bell, but it seemed the teachers' favorites usually got the privilege. My turn never came.

In the classroom we sat at desks that consisted of a wooden top and bench seat held in place within a black cast-iron framework. The seats were locked together in front-to-back rows, and there was a small wooden sidesaddle box on one side of the desk where we could put supplies. Each desk had an inkwell, but we used pencils rather than pens and ink. We each had an assigned seat and sat together by grades.

The first grade took up almost a whole row of seats on the left side of the classroom as we faced the front. When the teacher was instructing one grade, the other grades were given an assignment to work on. The task could be an art project, a workbook or a reading assignment. Sometimes the teacher addressed two classes at the same time, and sometimes the older students were asked to help students in the lower grades. The older students would stand next to us as the teacher was explaining something and check our work, or help us if we were having trouble completing an assignment.

Sometimes students sat in a circle using flash cards to drill each other in math or reading. We learned to read using

"Bill and Susan" and "Dick and Jane" readers. Bill and Susan had a dog named Perky, while Dick and Jane's dog was Spot and their cat was called Fuzzy. I remember the good feeling I had when I found that I could read words that told a story – even if it was a simple story like: "Look, look, see Fuzzy run and jump. See Spot chase Fuzzy. Dick and Jane laughed and laughed."

Initially I had some difficulty learning to read. But we drew names for a gift exchange at Christmas, and the teacher drew mine. She gave me a Golden storybook for Christmas and told me to use it to learn to read better. Most of the other kids got toys, and I was more than a little disappointed with my book. As it turns out, this was probably the best gift I could have received. My mother made me read the book over and over to her while she was working in the kitchen, and soon I could sound out all the words and read smoothly through the book. This extra help put me over the edge, and by the time I was in third grade the teacher enlisted me to help other students with their reading.

Discipline was very stern in the Big Springs School. In retrospect, I suppose strict discipline was necessary where a teacher was expected to teach four grades in a single room. However, it seemed to me that most of the kids, like me, were scared to death of the teacher.

One of the rigid rules was that we had to use the bathroom before school or during recess, not during class time. If a student made the mistake of asking the teacher if he could go to the restroom during class time, the teacher humiliated him with a loud berating in front of the entire classroom. She recited a lengthy lecture about using the restroom before school or during recess and not during class time. I guess you could say she scared the piss out of some of the kids, as some opted to wet their pants rather than ask the teacher if they could use the restroom. Of course this led to public humiliation anyway. If a student was allowed to go to the restroom but didn't return in what the teacher felt was an appropriate time interval, there would be another lecture. Most discipline was done in a very public way.

When learning to write letters and numbers, we had to do a lot of practice exercises with those big fat pencils that students were issued. We had to carefully print letters between lines on the paper. I remember how difficult it was for me to keep between the appropriate lines, and how hard it was to remember the difference between upper and lower case letters. I always had difficulty remembering the difference between a lower case b and a lower case d.

Sometimes I realized right away that I had used the wrong letter or made a letter backwards, but it wasn't an easy thing to correct a self-detected error. That's because one of the teacher's rules was that we were not to use erasers. If we made an error, we were to leave it on the page and keep going. The teacher enforced this rule by giving us pencils without erasers and confiscating all erasers in our possession.

It was at this point that I learned the truth behind the saying that necessity is the mother of invention. Lacking an eraser, I discovered that a rubber band could serve as a fine eraser substitute. When the teacher wasn't looking, I would reach down into the sidesaddle box and pull out a big fat rubber band that I had found there. I also looked around to make sure the teacher's tattletales weren't watching. The rubber band worked as well as any eraser, and the soft lead in our big fat pencils was easy to erase. After making the correction, I would carefully drop the rubber band back into the sidesaddle box for future use.

The blackboard (which was actually black) had lines on it just like the lines on some of the paper we used. On occasion we stood at the blackboard and practiced drawing letters neatly between the lines. This was difficult because, whether on paper or blackboard, being neat was never easy for me. My handwriting has always been messy. My letters and numbers always seemed crooked, and I was continually being chastised for poor penmanship.

There were also a number of unspoken, unspecified rules at the Big Springs School that I learned by trial and error. I learned one of them one day while playing on the tall slide in the schoolyard, which I particularly enjoyed. I decided that it would be cool to roll the red kickball down the slide in front of me. I climbed the slide with kickball in hand and sat down at the top. I was preparing to release the ball, when I heard Valerie behind me say, "Hmmm.....I'm going to tell teacher."

"About what?" I inquired.

"You're not supposed to roll the ball down the slide," Valerie said, with no small amount of haughtiness in her voice.

I decided that this was a rule that Valerie had made up on the spot, so I did what any red-blooded boy would do. I stuck my tongue out at her and rolled the ball down the slide with great ceremony. I quickly followed the ball down and went about the business of playing until the bell rang announcing the end of recess.

As I entered the classroom, the teacher was waiting just inside the door. I didn't see her until she grabbed me by the ear and pulled me out of line. That's when I knew Valerie had been true to her word; she had ratted me out for violating the "no balls down the slide" rule. In keeping with standard protocol, I got a very loud public scolding at the front of the classroom. All the while the teacher was holding me painfully by the ear. In the course of the lecture, I was informed that sticking my tongue out at someone was the most despicable, filthy thing a boy could do – right up there next to mass murder and torturing babies. I don't remember the teacher mentioning anything about rolling the ball down the slide, so I don't know to this day if that was really against the rules, or if Valerie had made it up on the spot.

When we got home from school that day, my brother Tom preceded me into the house and apparently couldn't wait to turn me in. As a general rule, if we got in trouble at school, it wouldn't be anything like the trouble we would find ourselves in when we got home. As I came in the house, my mother called me aside and asked me what I had done. When I explained the circumstances, she didn't discipline me. She just said that I shouldn't stick my tongue out at people, and that was the end of it. I thought I had ducked a bullet on that one.

For the record, I always used the restroom during recess, and I didn't roll another ball down the slide or stick my tongue out at anyone for the rest of my time at Big Springs Elementary School. For the most part I was a compliant kid, and the last thing I wanted to do was to come to the attention of the teacher, whom I viewed as something of a dragon.

Like most kids, I considered lunchtime one of my favorite parts of school. For several years we carried a metal lunch box with a thermos, but the average life expectancy for a thermos in the first and second grade was about a week. In those days thermoses came with a glass insulator lining that was extremely fragile. It was always just a matter of time until we would drop the thermos or the entire lunch box, breaking the glass lining and rendering the thermos unusable.

I can still recall the jingling sound a thermos made after the glass lining had been broken. When I heard that sound, I knew I wouldn't be having soup or milk with my lunch for a while, and I knew I was due for a "be more careful" lecture when I got home from school. My only consolation was that Tom seemed to break his thermos as often as I did. When we got older, lunch boxes were no longer cool, so we went to disposable paper sacks. This probably saved the family a small fortune in thermoses alone.

A typical school lunch consisted of an apple or orange; a peanut butter or fried egg sandwich, a hot dog wrapped in a pancake, a hardboiled egg and, sometimes, a cookie. On those rare occasions when we had an intact thermos, it might contain milk, chocolate milk or alphabet soup.

Like the other kids in the first grade, I often had difficulty peeling the orange that sometimes came in my lunch box. When I tried to peel one, it took forever, and the orange was usually reduced to a sticky, shredded mess in the process. The alternative and preferable technique for consuming an orange was to bite a hole in the peel and suck out as much juice as we could. When we couldn't extract any more juice from the hole, we would insert our fingers into the hole and tear the orange open.

It was still too difficult to separate the fruit from the peel, so I usually held the pieces to my face and chewed. This couldn't have been a pretty sight to watch, and it made a huge mess, but it was standard procedure in the first grade. To minimize the environmental impact, we usually ate our orange over the wax paper our sandwich had been wrapped in. For the rest of the day you could spot the kids who had oranges in their lunches because their chins and shirts told the story. I remember how sticky the orange juice was on my hands, arms, face and down my neck. It didn't seem to occur to any of us to wash it off. If we made too much of a mess of ourselves, the teacher ordered us into the bathroom to wash up.

Recess was another favorite part of school. At Big Springs we often played group games like dodge ball or kick ball. The boys usually played with boys, and the girls usually played with girls. Many games began by using a stick to draw two lines about 20 feet apart in the dirt of the school-yard. Someone would be designated as "it" and was required to stand in the no-man's-land between the two lines. Everybody else lined up behind the lines on one side or the other.

When the "man in the middle" gave the signal, everybody ran across the no-man's-land to get behind the other line drawn in the dirt. The man in the middle tagged as many runners as he could before they reached safety behind the opposite line. Sometimes the tagging was done with a kick-ball as a form of dodge ball. Once tagged, the runners had to stand to the side until the game was over. The game continued until everybody was tagged, and the last person tagged was considered the winner. This particular game was called "Black Man," but it didn't enter my mind until many years later that the name of the game probably had racist origins or connotations. Most of us at Big Springs had never seen a black man.

Our schoolyard didn't have a lawn or basketball court, but this was not a problem since most of the games we played only required a ball and a stick to draw lines or circles in the dirt. The schoolyard had plenty of dirt, a slide, a teeter-totter and a swing set – what more could we have asked for?

While the boys and girls usually played separately, we did play together for Annie-Annie-Over and Army. Annie-Annie-Over was played around the storage shed behind the school. The players divided into two teams and gathered on opposite sides of the shed. Someone with a kick ball called "Annie-Annie-Over" and threw the ball over the shed. If someone on the other team caught the ball before it hit the ground, the whole team ran around the shed, and the one who caught the ball threw it at the other team members. Anybody hit or tagged with the ball would be "out" and had to stand aside until the next game. The game was won when everybody on one team was "out."

Girls also played Army with the boys, but boys and girls played different roles. The boys were always soldiers, and the girls were always nurses. The boys would go out and pretend to shoot at each other or an imagined enemy. If a soldier suffered an imaginary injury, he reported to the girls who nursed him back to health. Rocks laid out on the ground formed crude squares, which defined hospitals. The girls required the injured soldiers to lie down in the hospitals while they made and applied bandages of grass and leaves. The girls tended to be bossy nurses, so the boys could hardly wait until they were declared well enough to return to battle.

My best friend at Big Springs was Johnny Bob Clark. He went by "Johnny Bob," and I thought it was neat that he had two first names. We often played together, and one of the things we did to entertain ourselves was to talk like adults. We walked around the schoolyard carrying on elaborate, serious conversations using all of the grownup words we could think of. No doubt, much of the time we used the words inappropriately, but it was fun. Johnny Bob was my first "best friend," and I have often wondered what became of him. We lost contact when my brother and I transferred from the Big Springs to the Grenada Elementary School.

GRENADA ELEMENTARY SCHOOL

While we lived in the Big Springs School District, my parents had reservations about the Big Springs School and eventually managed to get Tom and I transferred into the Grenada School District. Three years later, David followed us into the

Grenada School, but Dan attended a new and improved Big Springs School. Big Springs School was about three miles east of our mailbox, and the Grenada school was about four miles west. We were almost on the line between districts. The Grenada school bus didn't come out to Big Springs where we lived, but Grenada was on Dad's way to work in Yreka, so it was easy for him to drop us off at school.

I was in the third grade when we started attending Grenada Elementary School. At the time, Grades 3 through 5 were taught in an old one-room church building across the street from a larger red brick school building that housed the rest of the grades. Shortly after we arrived at Grenada Elementary, work started on a new school building, and within a year we moved into a modern new building with only two grades per classroom.

The photos on the left are from a page in the only yearbook Grenada Elementary School ever produced while we were attending. It was published in 1953 to commemorate the construction of the new school building. As a third grader, I modestly labeled all photos in the yearbook that included me with "ME" and drew an arrow to my picture to make sure nobody missed it. The upper right photo shows the 3rd, 4th and 5th grades on the steps of the church building where we attended classes until the new building was constructed. The church classroom is mentioned in the following poem that was written by students and included in the yearbook:

*"In an old, white church, with a tall, wide door
The third, fourth and fifth go to school with Mrs. Rohrer.
Some children come with Mrs. Collins on a big yellow bus
Others live in Grenada and got to class without a fuss.
With programs and parties we've tried to share our fun
And to learn to respect the rights of everyone."*

The yearbook also included brief statements that were written by each student about the things we liked to do. Tom wrote, "My name is Tommy Nelson. I have been president and secretary of our club. When the boys had the bulletin board to decorate we had the best display of airplanes and drawings. I'm looking forward to swimming and fishing this summer but this has been a good year in the fifth grade. When my school days are over I hope to be a jet pilot."

Being younger and considerably less articulate, I wrote, "I am Charles Nelson. Tom is my brother. We live in Big Springs."

First Row: Robert Pratt, Berry Mudgett, Billy Kent, Raymond Hogan, Charles Nelson, Bobby Bopp.
Second Row: Linda Swank, Maria Capovilla, Arlene Sears, Ara Mae Gray, Kay Crutchfield.

Some of the other students' submissions to the yearbook provide a bit of nostalgic humor and insight into rural life in Siskiyou County in the early 1950s:

"I am Judy Ann Iten. I play the accordion and take dancing lessons. I started to wear glasses this term."

Joe Helwig wrote, "I live on a farm. I have a calf and a pig that I hope to take to the county fair."

"Carl Truttman is my name. I am president of the Good Citizen and Bird Club now. I have a dog named Lady. It is easy to raise a dog on a ranch."

"My name is Billy Kent. I hadn't missed a day of school until I caught the mumps. Arlene had them first."

"My name is Stanley Sears. Sometimes we sing without the piano, and other times Mrs. Rohrer plays on an old out-of-tune piano but we sing just the same. I am raising a pig for the county fair."

"I am Fred Rose. I was born June 12, 1942 and I don't know what the world looked like then but it's O.K. now. School is O.K., too. Tom and I are in the school band. We belong to the 4-H too."

"My name is Janice Massaro. I like reading and drawing and writing poems. My hair is the prettiest kind of red, my teacher says."

"I am Gene Freeman. I live on a farm on the Montague road and ride to school on the bus. I belong to the 4-H. Fred and I are traffic officers right now, to see that children look both ways before crossing the road."

"My name is Patricia Jo Tourville. The subject I like best is arithmetic. I liked giving programs for the PTA. My class gave a talk on plants in September. Some of the sweet potatoes we started then are still growing. I am going to be a housewife or a model when I grow up."

"Arlene Sears is my name. I like learning my three tables. I like board work best of all. I made a clay dish that looked like a leaf."

"My name is Mary Ellen Facey and I am first on the fourth grade roll. My class is the largest in the room. All together we started the term with thirty-three and will end it with thirty-six if Don Osborn does not come back. There are many things I like about school. Right after lunch we sing and then the teacher reads to us. Some of the stories are exciting and Mrs. Rohrer makes them exciting. I like that period best."

The first and second graders also contributed statements to the yearbook:

Karen Gamma wrote, "I have a baby dog. I have a baby cat. I have a baby hen."

Billy Zentz wrote, "We have a cat that kills our chickens."

Pat Collens wrote, "I have a horse. He is brown and white. I like to ride him. He is a good horse. I like him."

Betty Truttman wrote, "Four big cattle trucks came to our house with cows in them."

Sandra Cook wrote, "I have a calf. I can lead him around the yard. I feed him milk."

Mark Root wrote, "I went up in the hills to make a camp fire. Bruce was with me."

Timothy Gomes wrote, "The best book I read was about a dog. I liked the book because it was a good dog story."

Living in the country and attending a small town school afforded us with many experiences that big city school kids don't have, such as when a skunk took up residence under the Helwig house. The Helwigs lived on a farm north of Grenada, and a skunk set up housekeeping in the crawl space under their house. The occasional skunk encounter is one of the minor disadvantages of country living. In the process of dislodging their boarder, it seems that the skunk sprayed the area pretty well. A little bit of skunk spray goes a long way, and the pungent odor soon filtered through the entire house, coating everybody and everything with essence of skunk.

The poor Helwig kids came to school smelling like skunk for a couple of weeks. It didn't matter how much they washed and scrubbed, the odor saturated the air in their home and reattached to them as quickly as they could wash it off. They apparently became accustomed to the smell, but the rest of us had to get used to it all over every day when they came to school. It must have been tough on the Helwig kids because the rest of us reminded them in no uncertain terms that they smelled like skunk.

The Grenada School was well equipped for a rural, small town school. We had a swing set, a merry-go-round and eventually even a sand box and a set of monkey bars. We had an all-dirt baseball field and a cement slab for a basketball court. My brother Tom played on the school baseball and basketball teams, and I played on the basketball team. I never liked baseball and had no desire to even try out for the team, although I eventually had my own baseball mitt and played recess baseball.

I was a long way from being a star basketball player at Grenada, but it was fun, especially when we would travel by car to play against another school. Usually the entire team fit in Coach Dunham's car when we went to an away game. We played against other small town schools such as Fort Jones, Hilt and Montague. Fort Jones had an outdoor court, but Montague built a new gymnasium with an indoor basketball court. Hilt also had an indoor gym, but it was an ancient wooden structure that reminded me of a barn as much as a gym.

One of my favorite basketball memories was when we were competing on our outdoor home court and I happened to sink a hook shot from close to half-court. I was as surprised as anybody that I made the shot, but I pretended it was no big deal. It was all the more sweet because my mother was there on the sidelines.

My brother Tom was the sports star of our family, and he did well in baseball and basketball, but he was especially good in football when he got to high school. Tom was one of the stars on the Yreka High School football team in his junior and senior years, and he also played football in college. Since he was traveling through school two grades ahead of me, I followed in his wake; and for the most part my identity in elementary and high school was that of being Tom's little brother.

Whether working or playing on the ranch or following in his tracks at school, it seems I was always trying to catch up or keep up with Tom. In high school, Tom became the student body president, but the best I could do was senior class president. While I couldn't keep up with Tom in baseball, basketball or football, I eventually found my own sports niche in gymnastics. It was a sport that had my name on it, and I was no longer in Tom's shadow. I lettered in gymnastics in high school and all four years of college.

Like every other kid, I complained about school but, in reality, my years at Grenada Elementary were good years. I had close friends during the school year and got a reasonably comprehensive education. My favorite part of school continued to be lunch and recess, but as I entered the upper grades, involvement in organized sports made it even more enjoyable. In the lower grades, recess consisted of various forms of tag and dodge ball similar to what we played at the Big Springs School, but the boys also played basketball and marbles, and the girls played hopscotch.

Playing marbles was a serious sport, and during "marble season" all the boys walked around with pockets bulging with marbles. There was great significance attached to the various kinds of marbles, and some were considered more valuable than others. Some marbles were multi-colored and opaque, and we called them "aggies" because they looked like they were made from agates. Others were clear glass with a color strip through the middle, and they were called "cats' eyes." Some marbles were actually ball bearings, so they were known as "steelies."

Everybody had a favorite marble that was his "shooter." A good shooter was a marble that was a "sticker." A sticker was a shooter that tended to stay in place after it struck the opponent's marble. If you could hit an opponent's marble and knock it away while your marble stayed put, you had a sticker. Stickers were big medicine in the game of marbles.

We played two basic games of marbles. The most common game was to chase and shoot at each other's marbles in the open. The other game was played by drawing a circle in the dirt and shooting at your opponent's marbles that were inside the circle. The objective was to hit any of the opponent's marbles in the circle with your shooter.

When we played marbles, there were many different rules. You could play for "keeps" or "no keeps." If you played for keeps, or "keepers" as we sometimes called it, you got to keep the opponent's marble when you hit it with your shooter. When playing for keeps, you also had to agree on whether you could keep the opponent's shooter, or if the opponent had the option of substituting any marble from his inventory rather than lose his favorite shooter. If you were playing for keeps and you could keep the shooter, you usually played with someone you knew was a lousy marble player, or you played with something other than your favorite shooter.

A common technique in marbles was something called "dropsies." Under certain rules of the game, when it was your turn to shoot, you could call "dropsies" and, instead of shooting at your opponent's marble on the ground, you could pick up your marble and try to drop it on your rival's marble from waist height. If you hit his marble by dropping your marble on it, it was counted the same as hitting it with a regular shot.

Another tactical consideration of the game was whether "fudgies" would be allowed. "Fudging" was when you moved your hand forward when shooting to give your marble additional speed or distance. A proper, non-fudgie marble shot required you to keep your knuckles fixed in one place on the ground while you used your thumb to project your marble forward. Fudging was considered cheating unless fudgies had been agreed to before the game started.

When entering into a game of marbles, both players negotiated the type of game as well as the rules of the game that was about to commence. Your skill as a marble player depended on how good of a shooter you had, how good you were at shooting it and how effectively you dickered over the rules. In order to successfully negotiate, you had to know your own strengths and weaknesses as well as those of your opponent.

If you were to listen to two kids about to enter into a game of marbles, it would sound something like this:

"Do you want to play marbles?"

"OK, keepers or no keepers?"

"Keepers, but you can't keep shooters."

"OK, but no steelies."

"OK, how about dropsies?"

"No dropsies or fudgies."

"OK, but you have to shoot first."

"OK, keepers but not shooters, no steelies, no dropsies, no fudgies and I shoot first."

With the rules negotiated, the game would begin with one player tossing his marble forward on the ground.

During the winter months when it was too cold, wet or muddy to go outside during lunch and recess, we often learned square dancing in the cafeteria. It was good exercise, and everybody participated. The teachers played square dance records and coached us through the moves. Square dancing was a popular activity for exercise as well as for social events. Sometimes 4-H clubs or other organizations would hold evening square dances at the school.

On occasion the Grenada schoolhouse was used for fundraising events, usually for the school or 4-H. One such event was a "box social." At a box social, the girls prepared a fancy meal and concealed it in a highly decorated box. The decorated boxes were auctioned off to the boys, who bid on them without knowing who made them or what was in them. The bidding tended to be based on how well the box was decorated. The hope was that someone who could decorate well might also cook well. The highest bidder got the box and shared the enclosed meal with the girl who made it. All of the proceeds of the bidding went to the cause for which the event was being held.

As a bashful kid, I found the box social events a little awkward. On the one occasion that I was persuaded to participate, my parents gave me some money to bid with, so I knew I wasn't going to starve, but I found the complex social interaction intimidating. I was rather timid to begin with, and now I had to figure out how to bid on a box and share a meal, which I may or may not like, with a girl I may or may not like. It was downright scary – I'd rather have gone to the cellar for a jar of jam after dark.

One of my classmates, Arlene, informed me which box she brought and told me it contained fried chicken. It was against all the rules of the event to divulge that information, so it was clear that she expected me to bid on her box and share the meal with her. I think she probably told several other boys the same thing, but I was on the spot. Fried chicken was an enticement, but Arlene was rather forward and a girl – a scary combination for a kid growing up in the country with no sisters.

I was spared from a tough decision when someone else – I think it was my brother Tom – out-bid me and got to share the meal with Arlene. I finally managed to place a winning bid on a box shortly before they were all gone. I shared fried chicken with an adult lady I had never seen before. It was scary, but not as scary as being seen with a girl.

Each year in December, we decorated our classrooms with a Christmas theme, and the students put on a Christmas program that involved singing and a play. All of the grades got to participate in one role or another. The program was scheduled for the evening of the last day of school before Christmas break, and all of the parents would be there. It was great fun for everyone. The program included traditional Christmas songs and carols. It was not a particularly religious event, but it was about Christmas, not a "Winter Festival," "Multicultural Fiesta" or some other more politically correct theme.

Whether we were attending Big Springs or Grenada, the school year always ended with a picnic. We looked forward to this with great anticipation because, not only was it a picnic, it marked the start of summer vacation. Often the school picnic took place on the banks of the Shasta River, but, wherever it was held, it involved swimming, potato

L-R: TOM, CHUCK & DAVID "STYLISHLY" DRESSED FOR SCHOOL IN 1955.

salad, fried chicken and soda pop. On the rare occasions we got rained out, it was a mild disappointment at best; school was still out for the summer.

Upon graduation from elementary school, all of the Nelson boys attended high school in Yreka. Because of our age spread, there was a Nelson boy attending Yreka High School for the better part of 16 years. High school was the launching platform from which each one of us set out to find our place in the adult world – a world much different from life at the end of a dirt road.

CHAPTER THIRTEEN

CHRISTMAS ON THE RANCH

Christmas is a special holiday for most Americans, and many family traditions build up around it. Christmas at the ranch was always special for the Nelsons, and rich family memories and traditions were centered on the Christmas season. Since we had moved onto the ranch just before Christmas in 1947, I have always thought of the ranch itself almost like a Christmas gift.

STOCKINGS FOR FOUR NELSON BOYS HANG FROM THE MANTLE WHILE A ROARING FIRE FILLS THE RANCH HOUSE WITH CHRISTMAS WARMTH.

One of the special events associated with Christmas was our annual trip into the surrounding mountains to chop down our Christmas tree. Living in the country, it was a natural thing to go into the woods to find and cut down our own tree. For many years I had no idea that most people bought pre-cut Christmas trees in a parking lot in front of a drug store. I suppose I thought everybody went to the woods to get a tree because that's where trees grow. After moving away from the ranch, I had the experience of selecting a pre-cut Christmas tree in a parking lot, and it was a disappointing experience by comparison. Even going to a Christmas tree farm to cut a tree is not the same as hiking into the wild woods to hunt for the perfect one.

Eventually, as a somewhat cynical adult, I decided that if I couldn't cut my own wild tree in the woods, a plastic tree was as good as a parking lot tree and much less of a fire hazard. Commercially harvested Christmas trees tend to be several weeks old and rather dry by the time you buy them. Today's plastic trees are less of a fire hazard and look authentic if you don't look too close. With some pine-scented chemicals added to your plastic tree, you can kick back in front of a wax-log fire, add some non-dairy creamer and artificial sweetener to your coffee-flavored drink and enjoy modern living.

We had plenty of trees on the ranch, but they were for the most part junipers or the willow and birch trees that grew down along the river. None of them could be considered a proper evergreen fir or pine Christmas tree. To find an authentic Christmas tree, we would drive into the snowcapped mountains surrounding Shasta Valley. Usually the excursion took us into the snow, and often we took a picnic lunch and made a day of it, sometimes with another family. It was a fun excursion that was one of our Christmas traditions.

On one such occasion I managed to get lost on the slopes of Mt. Shasta. I had set out on my own to find the perfect tree but paid more attention to the trees than the trail I was following. When I tried to find my way back, nothing looked familiar. I wasn't lost in a life-threatening kind of way, as I knew I could always hike 15 miles downhill and find civilization. However, I still recall the feeling of panic that threatened to overcome me when I realized it was getting dark and I had no idea where I was relative to everybody else. The woods had suddenly turned ominous and unfriendly. I backtracked and eventually found the correct trail that led me back to family. The experience taught me to pay attention to the landmarks when hiking in unfamiliar country.

SHOPPING FOR PRESENTS

In the early years on the ranch we often drove into Oregon to do our Christmas shopping. Yreka was the closest town for shopping in California but, in those days, it had a rather limited selection of stores. Oregon was only about a 60-mile trip from the ranch, and since it didn't have sales tax, our money went further. We usually shopped in downtown Medford, where there were many more stores than back "home" in Yreka.

The Christmas shopping experience began when my parents gave each of the older kids some money and told us to meet them back at the car at a particular time. The younger kids would stay with the parents, but Tom and I launched out on our own. We wandered from store to store trying to figure out what to buy for our brothers and parents. At the appointed hour we met at the car with bags of goodies, which we carefully guarded from prying eyes. From shopping day to Christmas Day, my brothers and I would taunt each other with, "I know something I won't tell," and cajole each other for hints as to what our gifts might be.

Buying gifts for your brothers isn't too hard because kids usually agree on what's "neat." Later in life, you learn that what looks really neat to a kid is not necessarily what an adult desires. The gifts we bought our parents were probably typical of what kids buy for their parents today, but they couldn't have been "neat" from an adult perspective. So far as I could tell, the folks always seemed happy to receive our carefully selected gifts, which were typically something like a ceramic black leopard or plaster of Paris Chinese heads.

HOLIDAY TREATS

Another thing that made the Christmas season special for the Nelsons was that Mom always did a lot of holiday cooking and baking. Christmas season was the only time of the year Mom made candy. Usually several days were dedicated to making candy, which included divinity, fudge with walnuts, rocky road and saltwater taffy. One of my favorites was candied orange and grapefruit peels.

A salt-water taffy pull was often part of the Christmas tradition. Mom gave us food coloring, coated our fingers with butter and showed us how to color and "pull" taffy to form interesting shapes and color patterns. It was fun, but we always burned our fingers as we dipped them into the molten taffy and competed to see who could make the most interesting shapes. I don't think we kids ever did anything together that didn't turn into some kind of contest. We were always striving to do something first, bigger, better or faster than the other brothers – competition was in our blood.

Mom was a good cook, and she also made cookies and pies during the Christmas season. My favorite cookies were refrigerator cookies because they tasted so good when dipped in milk. When I was older, I found they tasted just as good dipped in coffee. Mom's Christmas pies included mincemeat, pumpkin, apple and sometimes home-grown rhubarb. On Christmas Eve we had a tradition of seafood – usually prawns, scallops and smoked oysters – with cheese and salami on the side. Dinner on Christmas Day was always special, and turkey was the main course. Christmas dinner was essentially a repeat of Thanksgiving dinner with Christmas decorations.

On Christmas Eve the folks would let us kids stay up late, hoping we would sleep late in the morning. Of course it never worked out that way. By Christmas Eve we were so wired and excited that sleep was next to impossible. Sometimes when we were really young, Dad would sneak outside after we had gone to bed and make a jingling sound with spoons in a glass milk jar. Mom told us that the sound was sleigh bells and that Santa must be outside. Of course this launched another quart of adrenalin through our veins, and there was no possibility of sleep after we actually heard Santa's sleigh bells. We never *really* believed in Santa Claus, but at the same time we didn't want to not believe in him – just in case.

We kids usually got the folks up well before daylight on Christmas morning. But once we had the folks physically upright, they weren't "officially" awake until they had their coffee. It seemed like it took forever for that coffee to perk on Christmas morning. We couldn't start opening the presents until the folks had their coffee mugs in hand, a fire was started in the fireplace and we were all assembled in the living room.

AT LAST, STOCKINGS AND PRESENTS

The festivities on Christmas morning began with opening the stockings. There were four sons, so four stockings were always hung from the fireplace mantel. Stockings were an important part of Christmas, and it was always fun to see them hanging empty as we waited impatiently for the arrival of Christmas morning. The look and feel of a stocking stuffed full of goodies is a special memory. Our stockings always included a candy cane, some tangerines and nuts. Inside we typically found several little toys or other interesting gifts like modeling clay, coloring crayons, smoked oysters, a can of Army surplus crackers and something really neat like a pocketknife, a compass, or a box of BBs or bullets

for our favorite hunting rifle, depending on our age.

After stockings we opened packages one at a time. It was always a special time that lasted most of the morning. Each kid got something special, usually after dropping numerous hints throughout December. With an open fireplace, we tossed the wrapping paper in and burned it up as we progressed through the packages. Mom provided breakfast, but we were usually too excited to eat much. When all of the packages had been opened, we carted our booty off to our room and began to play with our favorite toys or games.

On Christmas Day, our father sometimes played with us as we tried out our new toys. This was special as it was about the only time that Dad played with us. If there was a toy that required competition or skill, we all played together, and it was great fun, even though the little brothers were hopelessly inept.

Some of my favorite toys as a kid included modeling clay, Tinker Toys, a bag of plastic soldiers, Lincoln Logs, an Erector Set, a sleeping bag, an electric train, a telescope, combat boots, a fishing pole and art supplies.

Once Tom got a chemistry set for Christmas, and we had great fun with it for a long time. As was the case with our cat-in-the-dryer endurance tests, our chemistry experiments were done safely beyond the supervision of parents. The written directions were far too boring, so we preferred to perform our own unscripted lab studies by mixing, boiling and blending different chemicals at random just to see what would happen. We awarded ourselves points for bad smells, unusual colors or unanticipated reactions among chemicals. If we made a test tube boil or fizz over, we considered it a successful experiment. Most experiments ended up with a black, hopelessly clogged test tube, which we invariably threw away. The tube usually smelled very much like Hell and would have been impossible to clean after we had mixed a number of haphazardly chosen chemicals in it and held it over a flame for several minutes.

Christmas memories on the ranch include the sight of bright and colorful Christmas tree lights framed in the ranch house window on a cold, jet-black winter night. There was always snow or frozen mud on the ground outside, but inside it was warm and filled with the smells of a fresh-cut Christmas tree, candy, pies and cookies. Excitement was in the air, and dreams ran rampant. The radio played Christmas carols, and Mom could often be heard singing along as she cooked and baked our Christmas treats. In the evenings Dad sometimes played the piano as we soaked up the warmth and soft, flickering light from the fireplace. It was a special time of year.

CHAPTER FOURTEEN

MOUNTAIN MAGGOTS AND COYOTES

If you want to know the essence of ignorance, look up the word "stupid" in the dictionary. It will no doubt say, "See sheep." It will probably cross-reference with "chicken," but we've already covered the nature and extent of chickens' stupidity. We had sheep on the ranch for most of my growing-up years, but I was never able to develop an appreciation for them as pets, livestock or meat. The only good thing about mutton or lamb chops was the mint jelly Mom always served with it.

Most of the time, our sheep ran wild on the range. It was common to see them dotting a hillside when you were out doing chores or taking a hike. Somewhere along the way I heard someone refer to sheep as "mountain maggots." This expression fit my sentiments exactly, so I took an immediate liking to the term. To this day I often refer to sheep as mountain maggots.

As a young child I enjoyed feeding young baby (bummer) lambs from a bottle, but once the lambs and I grew up, my opinion of sheep changed. Sheep are dumb as a stick, and when they are no longer cute little lambs, they are just dumb sheep. It's a real pain to protect them, both from predators

and the self-inflicted consequences of their feeble-minded-
ness.

In the spring we had to round up the sheep and put them
into pens so the ewes could have their lambs in a protected
environment. Baby lambs on the range tend to end up as
coyote food, and a ewe that's down while giving birth is
likely to meet the same fate. Coyotes are opportunists, and
sheep give them lots of opportunities.

Herding sheep is similar to herding cattle except it doesn't
smell quite as bad and it's less messy. Cows make cowpies;
sheep make pellets. A nervous sheep makes more pellets
than a calm sheep, but the pellets don't stick to your shoes
like a cowpie does – especially a nervous cow's cowpie.

Herding sheep can be somewhat more difficult than herding cattle because sheep are so stupid they never figure out
where you want them to go, and they are always scared spit-
less. Sheep are very much like chickens in that they tend to
be both dumb and "chicken." When some sheep get really
nervous, they faint. When a sheep fainted and dropped in
its tracks, I would get my hopes up, thinking it was dead,
but pretty soon it would jump up and continue being dumb
and scared. I was forever trying to keep the herd going in
the right direction, and the sheep were forever trying to find
a new direction. It helped to keep the lead sheep going in
the right direction because, like cattle, they usually follow
the leader – but not if they don't want to for any number of
reasons incomprehensible to humans.

When you are herding sheep, it's common for one to try to
take an unauthorized side trip while you have the main herd
headed in the right direction. The fact that they are always
scared of you is a double-edged sword. It works against
you because you never know when one is going to bolt from
the herd and run the wrong way. It works for you because

you can throw a rock so it lands in front of the sheep, and it will scare the runaway into turning around and scampering back to the flock.

With practice, you can herd sheep reasonably well with a handful of rocks. It's different with a cow. If one bolts from the herd and starts running in the wrong direction, you can throw all the rocks you want, but it won't turn the cow. You are going to have to outrun it or flank it until you can get in front of it and head it back in the direction you want it to go. But with sheep, a timely and well-thrown rock will often keep it headed in the right direction. As with chickens, sometimes stupid and scared is a good combination.

SHEARING SHEEP

Most people know that wool comes from sheep. As with cows and milk, and with chickens and eggs, sheep don't voluntarily give ranchers their wool out of gratitude for the loving care provided them by their pal, the rancher. You have to wrestle the stupid critters to the ground and shave it off. We usually sheared our sheep in the late spring. This way the sheep would go into the summer with a short "haircut" and be more comfortable during the hot months. A sheared sheep's haircut is a lot like the one a Marine recruit receives. It's not neat or pretty; it's a close shave. In the olden days ranchers used a sharp scissors-like device to shear the sheep, but today they use large electric clippers.

Shearing sheep takes a certain amount of expertise, and my folks preferred to hire someone to do it for them. Mr. Griswold was one of the best sheep shearers in our vicinity, and he was usually the man who did it for us. I liked it when he came because he was a nice and gentle man, and I was a friend of his sons Tim and Tom. Mr. Griswold was a man of many skills as he was also the county trapper and a square-dance caller.

When the sheep were to be sheared, Mr. Griswold set up where we had electricity, and we brought the sheep to him. This was usually done in the evening after he had spent his day working as a trapper. He could usually cut the fleece off in one piece, and the ugly, wool-less sheep was sent on its way looking rather naked and confused. The wool was bundled up and sold.

Sometimes the sheep got cut in the process of getting sheared. Sheep are not particularly cooperative, and minor cuts are not uncommon. The standard medicine for nicks and cuts was something called "sheep dip." Although it was used to protect the sheep from infections and insects, sheep dip was a horrible substance. It was a black, oily liquid that had a smell that could gag a maggot. You could smell sheep dip up-wind a mile away. I hated that stuff, but if you had sheep, you had to have sheep dip.

One particular sheep was a real pain in the butt. I mean that in a literal sense. This guy would hang around the barn with a real bad attitude. As long as you were looking at him, he was OK, but if you turned your back on him, he would charge you and butt you in the butt. It was just like you might see in a cartoon, but instead of seeing the stars that you see in cartoons, you felt real pain.

I was pretty young when this particular sheep was around. My first encounter with him was when I was playing around by the barn. There was a rope hanging in a loop from the roof of the barn. It ended about two feet from the ground, and I found that if I placed a board across the bottom of the rope loop, I could use it as a swing. This was fun for a while, but I then found that I could lie on my stomach across the board and swing around with my eyes closed and pretend I was flying.

This was great fun too, but while doing this, I was paying no attention to my surroundings. While I was focused on "flying" with my eyes shut, the renegade sheep came into the barn without my notice. As I was lying across the board on my stomach with my head projecting in one direction and my butt in the other, the sheep identified a target and marked the range and elevation. The first indication I had of the sheep's presence was when I felt a horrendous impact on my rear end that knocked the wind out of me. As I lay grunting and gasping on the ground, I saw the sheep with his ears back standing defiantly a few feet away. When I regained my breath and composure, I collected no small number of rocks and sent this bully on his way.

I was not the only one to "get it in the end." My mother told me that she was irrigating the field near the barn when she had a close encounter with the same sheep. She was on the edge of the ditch on her hands and knees opening an outlet so the water would flow better. This apparently presented a target the sheep could not resist, and he butted her in the backside, knocking her into the ditch. Because of my young age, I don't know what became of this particular sheep, but I can assure you that, if I were older, he would not have had the opportunity to die of natural causes.

TRAPPING WITH MR. GRISWOLD

Mr. Griswold – I think his first name was Clarence – had a significant influence on me as I approached high school age. At Grenada Elementary School, Tim Griswold and I were good friends. Sometimes we would stay overnight at each other's homes. Tim had an older brother Tom and two older sisters that I didn't know well. When I stayed overnight with the Griswolds, Tim, Tom and I had adventures that usually involved long hikes.

Mr. Griswold probably didn't have a good education, as we would think of an advanced academic education today. However, he was intelligent and rich in practical country knowledge. He was the county trapper, which meant he responded to predator complaints from ranchers. He was very knowledgeable about nature, and I loved to talk to him. He was not scary or hard to talk to as so many grown-ups were, and I learned a lot from him.

In addition to being a sheep shearer and a trapper, he was a square dance caller. The Griswolds belonged to a square dance club, and Mr. Griswold was one of the "callers." A square dance caller is the person who sings or calls out the moves during the dance. He tells you when to *dosey doe* and when to *allemande left*: *"All join hands and circle the ring, stop where you are and give your honey a swing. You swing that little gal behind you, then you swing your own."* On one occasion I went with the Griswolds to a meeting of their square dance club, but it was all too advanced for my elementary school skills.

My favorite times with Mr. Griswold were tagging along with him when his trapping rounds brought him to our ranch. We always had a problem with coyotes, as they would often kill calves and sheep on the ranch. I loved it when Mr. Griswold came by because he always took me with him. As we went about the ranch, he would explain what he was doing and why he was doing it, and tell stories about his experiences as a trapper.

He would scan the hills for signs of fresh digging that indicated a possible coyote den. He would ask me if there was a dead cow anywhere because he liked to set traps around dead animals, which were sure to attract coyotes.

When he found a suitable place to set out traps, he dug a shallow depression in the ground, set the trap and placed it in the depression. He put a piece of cloth over the face of the trap and used a screened box to shake light dirt and debris over the trap until it was covered. The cloth prevented dirt from filling in under the trap's pan, so the trap would spring shut when an animal stepped on the pan. Next he sprinkled dry grass and debris over the top until it looked just like the surrounding area. Each trap had a 6–foot chain on it, and he would secure the chain to a stake in the ground as far from the trap as the chain would reach. The stake was usually driven down in the middle of a sagebrush, if one was handy, to conceal it. He then covered the chain with dirt and debris until it too was invisible.

Finally he would open a jar of coyote bait, which was a black, greasy substance that smelled as bad as sheep dip, but different. It was his special recipe he made himself, and he said the key ingredient that made it work so well was seal oil. He would take a twig and dip it into this bait until he had a small dollop of the smelly goo adhering to the end of the stick. He then carefully placed the stick in the base of a clump of sagebrush or bronco grass near the trap. He placed it in such a way that if the coyote was sniffing for it, his feet would likely be over the trap. When he was done, we stepped back and surveyed the site. The steel trap was absolutely invisible, and the scent trap was set.

Mr. Griswold said his coyote bait was foolproof, and he was right. He would return to the ranch at least once every week or so when we had traps out, and we checked the traps together. In all, we caught several coyotes and one badger on the ranch. He carried a pistol and quickly dispatched the coyote before we removed him from the trap. He was a superior shot with his pistol and demonstrated this by nailing a rattlesnake at 15 feet on one occasion.

When we had a dead cow to work with, Mr. Griswold used a different technique to kill coyotes that were attracted to the scene. He had a spring-activated trigger device that looked like a wire frame wrapped in sheep wool. A .30-.06 cartridge could be mounted in the center of the frame in such a way that it didn't protrude above the sheep wool. The trigger device had a stake on one end, and it would be pounded several inches into the ground until it was firm and just the wool-covered trigger device was exposed about three or four inches above the ground. He usually installed this device in a clump of grass. Once the device was in place, he set the internal spring mechanism and carefully installed a .30-.06 cartridge that had a live primer but didn't have any gunpowder or a bullet in it. In place of gunpowder, the cartridge was filled with cyanide powder. Finally he would smear some of his foolproof coyote bait on top of the wool that covered the trigger device.

It was an ingenious device that worked very effectively. The coyote came into the area, attracted by the cow corpse. It smelled the irresistible coyote bait and tracked it to the wool sticking out of the ground. It would sniff at it, lick it and then place its mouth over the wool and give it a tug to try to lift it up. The upward tug released the trigger mechanism and set off the cartridge primer, blowing the cyanide powder directly into the coyote's mouth. The farthest the startled coyote could get before it dropped dead in its tracks was about 50 yards.

Keeping the coyote population in check is a necessary thing around agricultural operations. Mr. Griswold was a gentleman and a gentle man who loved the outdoors and nature, but he was very good at killing coyotes. It was his job, and he was paid for it. Many people don't understand the need to keep predators in check and disapprove of such things. They might feel different about predator control if coyotes were to periodically sneak into their bank account and run off with a $500 bill.

COYOTE KILL: THIS PHOTO WAS TAKEN BY SEDG NELSON IN 1974. A NOTE ON THE BACK INDICATES BOTH THE COW AND HER CALF WERE KILLED BY COYOTES WHEN SHE WAS DOWN GIVING BIRTH. THE NOTE SAYS COYOTES TOOK "4 TO 6 CALVES A YEAR FOR THE LAST 5 YEARS."

Today steel traps are outlawed, and the full-employment act for lawyers probably precludes the use of the cyanide devices. I don't know how ranchers keep coyotes under control today without going bankrupt. One method is to fly around in a helicopter and shoot them, but that has to be terribly expensive. Coyotes are largely nocturnal, so hunting them by helicopter during the day would probably have limited success.

The time I spent with Mr. Griswold was interesting, educational and fun for me. He was one of the few adult males who made me feel comfortable. He was even-tempered, friendly and non-threatening. He seemed to respect me and was always teaching me something while talking about his experiences with animals.

CHAPTER FIFTEEN

MEMORIES AT THE END OF A DIRT ROAD

As we're growing up, certain memories, events and experiences take on a significance that follows us into adulthood. They may not always be major, life-changing events, but somehow they become part of who we are because they are parts of who we were. Such experiences add flavor and texture to life as we live it, and they shape the person we will become in ways we usually don't recognize at the time. Following are some of the memorable vignettes and experiences that were part of growing up at the end of a dirt road.

WHERE'S DAVID?

Deer season was an important annual event. In the early years on the ranch, our parents hunted to help put food on the table. In later years Tom and I took up deer hunting as part of the passage from boyhood into manhood. When the other kids at school started talking about the bucks they bagged, it was time to take up serious hunting so that we would also have bragging rights during recess. While we sometimes hunted around the county, Tom and I each got deer right there on the Nelson Ranch.

When we were young, sometimes the folks got us up early in the morning, and we drove up into the hills ringing the Shasta Valley to hunt deer. On one such occasion we wound our way high up on the west side of Whaleback Mountain – part of the Cascade Range on the east side of the Shasta Valley. The road was probably the remains of an old logging road, but it had not been used for logging in years. Somewhere high on the side of the mountain in the middle of some tall trees, Dad parked the car, and he and Mom took their rifles and set out to get a buck. Tom, David and I were left behind with strict instructions not to leave the car. David was probably around 5 years old at the time, so Tom and I must have been about 12 and 10 years old respectively.

After the folks had been gone an hour or so, we were getting pretty bored sitting in the car. We had pushed, poked, punched and annoyed each other to the point that there was nothing left to do. At about this time it started to snow a little, and Tom decided it might be fun to play hide and seek. We got out of the car and played a few rounds of hide and seek in the woods around the car. By this time, the snow was coming down pretty hard and starting to stick to the ground. We decided to play one more round of hide and seek, and David was "it." Tom and I were going to hide, and little Dave would have to come looking for us – in the woods in a snowstorm.

According to the rules of hide and seek, Dave had to count to 10 slowly while Tom and I lit out to hide. We liked it when David was "it" because he was fairly easy to hide from, especially since we had honed "ditching the little brother" to an art form. We did a pretty good job of hiding, and the snow was covering our tracks almost as quickly as we laid them down. After a lengthy period of time, we grew weary of crouching behind trees in the snow, so we made our way back to the car. By now it was snowing quite hard and visibility was poor, so Tom and I climbed into the car to keep warm. We figured that hiding in the car was a good idea anyway – David would never find us there.

Not too much later, Mom and Dad, coated with snow, arrived back at the car and found Tom and I inside, warm and cozy. When they opened the car door, they looked at us, looked at each other then said in unison, "Where's David?" Tom and I shrugged our shoulders and explained that we were playing hide and seek, and since David was "it," he was "out there looking for us."

As an adult looking back, I can understand my parent's reaction to this news. Their 5-year-old son was by himself in the woods in the wilderness in a blizzard – a reasonable cause for concern. At the time, however, as a kid on the winning side of hide and seek, I thought their reaction was unusually extreme.

Both Mom and Dad made it *crystal clear* to Tom and me that we had done a dumb thing by losing our little brother in the woods during a snowstorm. Soon we were all walking in widening circles around the car shouting, "DAVID, DAVID" as loud as we could. Tom and I had to stay close to the car, but Dad made wider circles while Mom kept an eye on Tom and me.

Before too long, Dad came back to the car with David, who was a bit wet and cold, but no worse for the wear. David thought he was in trouble because everybody was hollering his name. He had been so intent on trying to find Tom and me out there in the woods that he had no time to worry about being lost.

It may have been snowing outside, but Tom and I didn't notice because we were in hot water for the rest of the day.

PICKING BLACKBERRIES

Blackberries are delicious, and they make great jams, pies and cobblers. We didn't have blackberry bushes on the ranch, but they grew wild in many places in Siskiyou County and especially along the Klamath River. For many years Mom took us kids blackberry picking at least once or twice during the summer.

Blackberry picking was usually an all-day event. Sometimes we would go with another family, but usually it was just Mom and the kids. I don't remember Dad ever going blackberry picking with us. Mom packed a picnic lunch, and it would be a day of work and play away from our normal chores.

Since blackberries grow best near water, picking blackberries often meant getting wet, so we usually picked blackberries in our swimming suits. Often we would stand in the river or a ditch in order to pick the big fat berries that hung out over the water.

Blackberry vines are covered with sharp thorns, so getting poked and scratched was an inevitable part of blackberry picking. We could eat all the blackberries we wanted along the way. Sampling the blackberries as we went helped us to judge what a ripe berry looked like. A ripe one was all black with no red or green showing. A green blackberry tastes as bad as a ripe one tastes good.

Mom would give each of us a coffee can or a small bucket, and send us out to fill it with blackberries. It was fun at first, but it eventually became a bit tiresome. When the bucket was full, we took it to Mom, who was also picking berries. She would inspect the contents of our buckets to make sure we had picked ripe berries. Then we dumped them into a large container, and Mom would send us off to fill our pails again.

At some point during the day, Mom called us in and we had our picnic lunch. It usually consisted of macaroni or potato salad, fried chicken and Kool-Aid, which we consumed as we sat on a blanket in a green field.

At the end of a good day of blackberry picking, we were tired and sleepy. Our hands and faces were stained red with blackberry juice; our fingers, arms and legs were covered with scratches; and our necks, backs and shoulders were well sunburned. It doesn't get any better than this in the country.

In my opinion the work was worth it because Mom always made a blackberry cobbler and maybe a pie or two within a few days of our expedition. Best of all, so far as I was concerned, was the blackberry jam Mom made. To this day I can't think of anything better than a slice of bread with peanut butter and Mom's homemade blackberry jam.

OH BOY, ROOT BEER!

In the early days on the ranch, money was scarce, so we didn't often get to have a treat such as a bottle of soda pop. We usually referred to soft drinks like Coke, root beer or orange soda as soda pop or just "pop." We didn't eat out very often, and it was a special treat when we could go to a café and order a hamburger and a milkshake or soda. The term "fast food" hadn't been invented yet, and we lived 15 miles from a town, so most meals were prepared and consumed at home. A 30-mile round trip for fast food would have ended up as slow food, so wild ducks and deer were as close to fast food as we came.

LIFE IS GOOD AT A RANCH PICNIC.
CHUCK ENJOYS AN APPLE AND SODA.

When I was young, my favorite soda was orange pop. I can still remember how good a cold orange soda tasted on a hot summer day. In the 1950s only beer came in metal cans. Soda always came in a glass bottle, and it was not sold out of a vending machine or in six-packs. At least that's the way it was in Siskiyou County. Soda was usually sold loose out of a red metal insulated box with the Coca Cola emblem on it. The box had a lid that was red, silver or white, and sodas of all kinds were inside, sitting in ice and water. You had to lift the lid and sort through the selection until you found the soda you wanted. The box had a bottle opener mounted on it, so you could immediately pop the cap off of your selection. Often the box of iced sodas was in front of a store or gas station, and you would take your selection inside to pay at the cash register. The "honor system" worked back then. The best soda to pick was one that was deep inside the ice and water because it was sure to be really cold.

When you are a kid, the effervescence of soda pop really burns your nose as you drink it. I can still remember the fizz in my mouth and sting in my nose when I drank my favorite orange soda. The effervescent quality of soda pop also releases gas after you swallow it. This released gas eventually manifests itself as a burp. If you tried to stifle the burp and let it pass quietly through your nose, it would burn the bejeebers out of your nasal passages on the way out. If, on the other hand, you released the gas through your mouth, you would spare yourself the pain in your nose and, as an added bonus, you could often produce a substantial, audible burp.

From the perspective of us kids, the production of gas (from whatever source) that could be released in audible form (from whichever orifice) was always a plus. The production of gas was a delightful byproduct of soda pop. This discovery led to burping contests for which points would be awarded based on the volume and/or duration of the burp. Extra points could be added for imaginative modulation of a burp. Our parents tried, with limited success, to discourage these burping contests. So remarkable was this linkage between drinking soda pop and burping that we began to refer to soda pop as "burp gas."

When we lived in the Red House on the ranch, Mom learned how to make homemade root beer. I have never been unduly fond of root beer, but it was nice to be able to have a soda pop once in a while, even if it was root beer. Often we added ice cream and made homemade root beer floats.

I don't remember the recipe, but Mom would mix the ingredients together in a large ceramic pot she called a crockpot. She then ladled the dark brew through a funnel into pop bottles, which we had saved for this purpose. She then placed a bottle cap on top of the bottle and pulled down on the handle of a bottle capper to crimp it tightly in place. The root beer at this stage was a sweet root beer-flavored liquid, but it was not yet effervescent. The bottles were then placed in the closet on the back porch, where they stayed until the yeast in the mixture fermented and produced gas that would provide the effervescence that was the essence of pop.

Once the gas had formed in the bottles, it tasted just like store-bought root beer. One of the clues that told us the gas had formed and the root beer was ready for drinking was the sound of bottles exploding in the closet. Apparently the gas-forming action was so strong that the pressure inside the bottle exceeded the strength of the pop bottle, and "POW," the bottle would explode, spraying glass and sticky, foaming root beer all over the closet. Whenever we took a bottle of root beer from the closet, we had to look out for broken glass and wash off the sticky remains of previously exploded bottles.

On one particular occasion when Mom was making home-made root beer, my brothers David, Tom and I were sitting around the kitchen table watching her ladle root beer into bottles. Mom had a sort of one-person assembly-line operation going. She ladled the root beer from the crock-pot into a bottle, placed a bottle cap on it, crimped it in place with the bottle capper and then set the capped bottle aside.

The table we were sitting around was typical early '50s vintage with chromed metal legs and a vinyl top with a red-and-white crackle pattern. We kids were all pretty young. Tom and I were sitting on our knees on chairs on one side of the table while little David, still in diapers, was standing on a chair next to Mom on the other side. We were all excited that Mom was making root beer and having our usual noisy good time.

As Mom was ladling the mixture into the bottles, some of it would spill and stream across the table toward Tom and me. If the root beer stream came in my direction, I shouted, "Oh Boy, root beer," and bent over to slurp up the sweet liquid from the surface of the table. If the stream went in Tom's direction, he shouted, "Oh Boy, root beer," and loudly sucked it from the table. It was great fun and somewhat of a competition to be the first one to claim title to a new stream and to snort it up before the other one could get to it.

At some point during this noisy competition, I spied a familiar golden stream flowing across the table in my direction. Feeling fortunate to have spotted it before Tom, I shouted, "Oh Boy, root beer," and quickly began to suck it up. At the same time, I heard Tom and Mom shouting, "WAIT! STOP!" It was immediately apparent to me that there was something dreadfully wrong with this particular stream of root beer. It tasted awful. As Tom and Mom began to laugh hysterically, I lifted my eyes and realized what had happened. The golden stream did not lead to the crock-pot; it led to David's diaper, which was just at tabletop height as he stood on a chair across the table.

I ran spitting and gagging for the bathroom, with Tom dancing and laughing behind me. I held my head under the bathtub faucet and ran cold water into my mouth while I rinsed and spat for several minutes. Tom and Mom had a good laugh out of it, but it took me a while to find the humor in it. David was too young to know what the hilarity was all about, but at least he got a diaper change.

To this day, that incident is a standing joke in our family. The full story hasn't been told in years, but everybody knows the punch line. Just say, "Oh Boy, root beer," at a Nelson family gathering, and everybody breaks out in laughter. Personally, I don't think it's all that funny; in fact, it leaves me with a bad taste in my mouth.

POPCORN AND THUNDERSTORMS

When our family first moved to Siskiyou County, before we settled onto the ranch, we lived for a short time in a housing project at the south end of Yreka. The houses were nothing fancy and had been built as temporary housing for the families of men who were returning to civilian life after the end of World War II. There were other families living in the projects, so Tom and I found children to play with.

It was in the housing projects that I learned about the "boogey man." The boogey man was never defined, but when I heard the other kids talking about him in hushed tones and with fear in their eyes, I knew he was some kind of bad guy. One day when a bunch of us kids were outside at play, we heard the distant rumble of thunder. I didn't recall having heard anything like this before, and it was rather ominous. The other kids stopped their play, looked to the sky and whispered, "The boogey man." It sounded rather spooky so I wanted to know exactly who and where this boogey man was. When I pressed the other kids for more information, they all pointed to some dark, foreboding clouds in the sky and indicated that the boogey man was up there. At about that time there was a blinding flash of lightning and an ear-splitting clap of thunder, followed by a heavy rumbling of the sort that rattles deep into your chest. Without a word, the kids took off running as fast as they could for their respective homes.

Tom and I hit the front door hard and ran into the apartment fully confident that the end was near. Mom had heard the thunder and was expecting us to come home, but when we dashed through the door at full speed and leaped into her arms with terror in our eyes, she couldn't help but burst out laughing. Tom and I could see that Mom didn't appreciate the extreme danger we were all in, so it looked like we were on our own. We ran for the bedroom and crawled under the bed as thunder pounded the house and hail pelted the roof.

Mom got down on her hands and knees and explained that the terrifying boom was just thunder and it wouldn't hurt us. However, when you hear thunder, unexpectedly, up close and personal for the first time, there are no words that can convince you that anything that fearsome and powerful is not dangerous. Finally, as the thunder continued and Tom and I were ricocheting off the walls in terror, Mom came up with a plan to calm our fears. She announced that she was going to make some popcorn. It worked like a charm. With our attention fixed on the fact that Mom was making popcorn, our obsession with the storm outside began to fade. Sure enough, before long we had popcorn to eat, and the storm was gone. Mom had saved the day.

What began as a maternal inspiration quickly became a tradition. After we moved onto the ranch, whenever a thunderstorm came on us, Mom always made popcorn for Tom and me to help us get through the storm. The storms were still scary, but popcorn was our refuge.

As we got older we became less afraid of thunderstorms but still appreciative of the popcorn diversion that came with them. On hot summer days Tom and I would scan the morning sky to see if thunderclouds might be developing over the mountains. If clouds were developing by 10:00 in the morning, we had a good chance of an afternoon thunderstorm. The knobby white tops of the thunderheads reminded us of the popcorn we could expect if a thunderstorm came our way. Sometimes we heard the faint sound of distant thunder and ran to report to Mom that it was time for popcorn. Mom reminded us that the storm had to be closer and louder to warrant the popcorn diversion.

In those days nobody had microwave ovens, and popcorn didn't come in pre-measured packages. Popcorn was made by pouring some popcorn kernels and oil into a pie tin or frying pan and heating them over a burner on the stove. It was hard to keep the popcorn from flying all over the place when it began to pop, so Mom would put a lid over the pan. Our excitement would build as we heard the muffled popping under the lid and the smell of popcorn filled the kitchen. After it was popped, Mom would melt butter to pour over the popped popcorn and top it off with a bit of salt from a shaker. Eventually Mom got a corn popper that kept the popcorn from spilling all over the place when it was cooked over the stove.

Thanks to the popcorn distraction, Tom and I got pretty good at predicting the weather, and we learned not to fear thunder and lightning. In fact, it was quite a disappointment when promising clouds failed to blossom into a proper thunderstorm or when a good storm missed the ranch.

THE NIGHT OF THE FIRE

The occasional summer thunderstorm was usually welcomed relief from the hot summer sun. Storms were especially welcomed if they brought a good rain. Most thundershowers were little more than enough to settle the dust, but occasionally we got enough rain to soak the pastures and justify turning off the river pump for a few days.

Thunderstorms often knocked the power out, sometimes for long periods of time, but more often they would cause the power to fluctuate. When a power fluctuation caused the lights to dim at the house, it was a signal that told us that the river pump had probably shut itself off. The slightest power fluctuation caused the pump to shut down. When this happened, we had to wait until the storm was over and then go down to the river to restart the irrigation pump – sometimes late at night.

During the summer, we frequently ate late in the evening because when Dad came home from work, he often headed out to work on a project somewhere on the ranch. He frequently stayed out until it was too dark to see. Mom didn't always know when Dad would come in for dinner, so she planned meals accordingly. It wasn't unusual to eat dinner as late as 10 p.m. Mom kept dinner warm and held us kids at bay until Dad came in, then we would all sit down and eat together. I found that imminent starvation was the best spice you could put on food. Mom was a good cook but, with a little starvation to stimulate your appetite, anything would taste good.

One summer evening, it was just about dark as we were finishing dinner. Outside there was the occasional lightning flash and rumble as a mild thunderstorm was passing over the ranch. Suddenly there was a bright flash of lightning outside, followed instantly by a tremendously loud boom of sky-splitting thunder. The noise pounded our ears for several seconds before trailing off. It startled all of us, and we remarked that it must have been a close one because the flash was so bright and the boom was loud and instantaneous. But since the power didn't go out, we didn't think anything more of it.

An hour or so later, well after dark, we heard the dog barking and noticed car headlights coming up the road toward the house. It was after 10 p.m., and we thought it was rather late for company, but we stepped out the front door to see who it was. As soon as we were outside, we saw a wall of flames coming over the top of the hill north of the house. We knew instantly that we had a lightning fire on our hands. The storm had passed, but it had been a dry storm with no rain to wet the grass and dampen the fire a lightning strike had started.

Our immediate goal was to protect the house, but there were other critical concerns. This particular year, Dad had planted barley in Field No. 5, and it was dry and ready for harvest. If the fire got to the barley, the flames would be unstoppable and the entire field would be lost. Dad had also rented a large combine for harvesting the field, and it was parked in the dry grass near the house and in the path of the fire. While Dad raced off to move the harvester to a safer spot, Tom and I grabbed shovels and headed up the hill to confront the fire.

For the most part the fire was burning the dry bronco grass that was so abundant on the ranch. Bronco grass burns easily, but a fire usually moves along so rapidly that it tends not to set trees on fire. With the shovels, it was fairly easy to beat out the flames and throw dirt on stubborn burning patches. Tom and I worked feverishly to stop the wall of fire in its tracks. Some neighbors, whose headlights we had seen earlier, had arrived and were beating out the flames to the east of us, so Tom and I worked our way west over the top of Eagle Peak, extinguishing the line of fire as we went.

The fire turned out not to be as serious as we first thought. While we initially feared that we might lose the house, some farm equipment and the field of barley, the fire ultimately did little serious damage. It was mostly confined to the bronco grass, and few juniper trees actually burned. The fire even spared most of the sagebrush. A Division of Forestry crew eventually showed up, and we all worked late into the night putting out hot spots.

The next day we could see the fire had left an ugly black path in its wake. There were still many sagebrush and juniper trees standing relatively unscathed in the midst of the blackened grass. About a half-mile from the house, along Nelson Road, we found the juniper tree that was the source of the fire. Lightning had split the tree in two, and the black path of the fire spread south and west from there.

Some of our neighbors who had come to help us put the fire out said they had to dodge rattlesnakes that were fleeing in front of the fire. Tom and I didn't encounter anything like that. It was a scary night for us, but not because of rattle-snakes. We had seen how rapidly a wildfire could move and, for a time, we believed we were fighting to save our home. It was an exciting night at the end of a dirt road.

POEM ON THE RANGE

While my father was viewed as the undisputed intellectual force in the family, Mom was far from being a backward country girl. Dad overshadowed Mom with his college degree and by force of his personality, but Mom's influence on us kids was no less significant.

One of the things I remember about her was her love of poetry. Bear in mind that she grew up BT (before television), and most of my years on the ranch were also BT. Many people today cannot imagine life without television, but it was not a life of idleness and deprivation. In those days entertainment was less visual and passive, and more audible and participatory. Radio, card games, reading, conversation and outdoor activities were a major part of entertainment and family life. We didn't miss what we didn't have, so we filled our minds and time with what we had.

Mom often recited her favorite poetry to us when we were kids. In fact, we often asked her to tell us a poem. It's difficult to imagine this today, but it was not unusual for us. Poetry probably sounds boring to a generation that turns to the cartoon channel for entertainment, but it didn't seem boring at the end of a dirt road. The rest of the country had TV long before it reached us on the ranch, but we in no way felt deprived.

Mom was a fan of the poet Robert Service and especially his poems about his experiences and the lore of the Klondike Gold Rush of 1898. Somewhere along the way, Mom had memorized a number of poems and among them were

Robert Service's "The Cremation of Sam McGee" and "The Shooting of Dan McGrew." I can remember several poems that she recited, but these were among our favorites. Even before we could understand all the words in these poems, we hung on every one and the story that came in rhyme.

Try to imagine what it was like as a BT kid to hear such poetry without being able to compare them to "Sponge Bob" or "The Simpsons."

The Cremation of Sam McGee

There are strange things done in the midnight sun
By the men who moil for gold;
The Arctic trails have their secret tales
That would make your blood run cold;
The Northern Lights have seen queer sights,
But the queerest they ever did see
Was that night on the marge of Lake Lebarge
I cremated Sam McGee.

Now Sam McGee was from Tennessee, where the cotton blooms and blows.
Why he left his home in the South to roam 'round the Pole, God only knows.
He was always cold, but the land of gold seemed to hold him like a spell;
Though he'd often say in his homely way that he'd "sooner live in hell".

On a Christmas Day we were mushing our way over the Dawson trail.
Talk of your cold! Through the parka's fold it stabbed like a driven nail.
If our eyes we'd close, then the lashes froze till sometimes we couldn't see;
It wasn't much fun, but the only one to whimper was Sam McGee.

And that very night, as we lay packed tight in our robes beneath the snow,
And the dogs were fed, and the stars o'erhead were dancing heel and toe.
He turned to me, and "Cap," says he, "I'll cash in this trip, I guess;
And if I do, I'm asking that you won't refuse my last request."

Well, he seemed so low that I couldn't say no; then he says with a sort of moan:
"It's the cursed cold, and it's got right hold till I'm chilled clean through to the bone.
Yet 'tain't being dead – it's my awful dread of the icy grave that pains;
So I want you to swear that, foul or fair, you'll cremate my last remains."

A pal's last need is a thing to heed, so I swore I would not fail;
And we started on at the streak of dawn; but God! he looked ghastly pale.
He crouched on the sleigh, and he raved all day of his home in Tennessee;
And before nightfall a corpse was all that was left of Sam McGee.

There wasn't a breath in that land of death, and I hurried, horror-driven,
With a corpse half hid that I couldn't get rid, because of a promise given;
It was lashed to the sleigh, and it seemed to say: "You may tax your brawn and brains,
But you promised true, and it's up to you to cremate those last remains."

Now a promise made is a debt unpaid, and the trail has its own stern code.
In the days to come, though my lips were dumb, in my heart how I cursed that load.
In the long, long night, by the lone firelight, while the huskies, round in a ring,
Howled out their woes to the homeless snows – O God! how I loathed the thing.

And every day that quiet clay seemed to heavy and heavier grow;
And on I went, though the dogs were spent and the grub was getting low;
The trail was bad, and I felt half mad, but I swore I would not give in;
And I'd often sing to the hateful thing, and it hearkened with a grin.

Till I came to the marge of Lake Lebarge, and a derelict there lay;
It was jammed in the ice, but I saw in a trice it was called the "Alice May."
And I looked at it, and I thought a bit, and I looked at my frozen chum;
Then "Here," said I, with a sudden cry, "is my cre-ma-tor-eum."

Some planks I tore from the cabin floor, and I lit the boiler fire;

Some coal I found that was lying around, and I heaped the fuel
higher;
The flames just soared, and the furnace roared – such a blaze you
seldom see;
And I burrowed a hole in the glowing coal, and I stuffed in Sam
McGee.

Then I made a hike, for I didn't like to hear him sizzle so;
And the heavens scowled, and the huskies howled, and the wind began
to blow.
It was icy cold, but the hot sweat rolled down my cheeks, and I don't
know why;
And the greasy smoke in an inky cloak went streaking down the sky.

I do not know how long in the snow I wrestled with grisly fear;
But the stars came out and they danced about 'ere again I ventured
near;
I was sick with dread, but I bravely said: "I'll just take a peep inside.
I guess he's cooked, and it's time I looked";. . . then the door I opened
wide.

And there sat Sam, looking cool and calm, in the heart of the furnace
roar;
And he wore a smile you could see a mile, and he said: "Please close
that door.
It's fine in here, but I greatly fear you'll let in the cold and storm -
Since I left Plumtree, down in Tennessee, it's the first time I've been
warm."

There are strange things done in the midnight sun
By the men who moil for gold;
The Arctic trails have their secret tales
That would make your blood run cold;
The Northern Lights have seen queer sights,
But the queerest they ever did see
Was that night on the marge of Lake Lebarge
I cremated Sam McGee.

In our busy world today, few of us take time to read or listen
to poetry, let alone memorize it. I was fortunate to have had
the opportunity to taste a bit of life when it was lived at a
slower pace – when there was time for poetry.

One day, under unusual circumstances, Mom met a kindred spirit at the ranch. For many years, Dad leased the lake and river to a duck-hunting club during duck season. It was an important source of income for the ranch. On many a cold fall morning I can remember waking to the sound of shotguns on the lake below the house. The club members came on weekends, holidays and Wednesdays to try for their bag of ducks.

The duck-hunting club was based in Mt. Shasta City, and some of the members were well placed citizens of Siskiyou County. I recall one cold morning when a duck hunter with a problem came knocking on our back door. He was well fortified against the cold with liquid spirits, but his shotgun had jammed in a serious way. He had come seeking the warmth of the house and to see if he could borrow some tools to repair his gun so he could continue hunting. Having braced himself against the weather with spirited drink, he was feeling no particular pain, but his frozen fingers were refusing to obey. In the cold with numb fingers and no tools, he had been unable to repair his shotgun, but he knew the house would provide the warmth, tools and eventually the dexterity he required to un-jam his gun.

Only Mom and we kids were home, but, in accordance with ranch hospitality, he was invited in and was provided the tools he needed. Mom and the half-frozen duck hunter engaged in friendly conversation as he dismantled his gun and laid the pieces out on the kitchen table. Mom made a pot of hot coffee strong enough to float a pistol and encouraged the duck hunter to drink lots of it as he puttered with his gun. While she told him the coffee would help warm him up, she was, no doubt, hoping it would counteract his "cold medication" as well.

At some point in the conversation it was determined that the duck hunter was also a fan of Robert Service. Before long he and Mom were trading off elaborate poetic recitations while his clumsy frozen fingers tinkered with his dismantled gun. Perhaps by nature or perhaps by virtue of his intoxication, the duck hunter waxed theatrical and enthusiastically bellowed the best of Robert Service so loudly he could be heard from anywhere in the house. Eventually the gun was repaired and the duck hunter disappeared into the foggy cold outside the back door. I remember this literary event as one of many brief but interesting cultural vignettes, featuring a drunk duck hunter and a hospitable ranch mom, at the end of a dirt road.

MO AND HOUND DOG

A ranch mom's life is not an easy one. In addition to cooking, cleaning, gardening and taking care of the kids, Mom was often called on to help with the ranch work Dad normally did, especially when he was away on business, which he was with some regularity. It was not uncommon for my mother and us kids to be alone on the ranch for a week or more while Dad was on a trip to Davis or wherever the Agricultural Extension Service sent him.

Sewing up holes in our clothes and ironing patches on the torn-out knees of her kid's pants would have been a full-time job for some mothers, but that was just part of Mom's busy days. Along with her household and yard chores, she fed the critters, milked the cows, changed the irrigating sets or did whatever needed to be done to keep the ranch going. We kids were given age-appropriate chores so we could help out as we grew up. To lighten her load, Mom often asked Tom or me to dry dishes while she washed them. When we were older, we often had to wash and dry dishes, but when we were little, we only dried them.

Like most normal, healthy kids, we grumbled when asked to help out, but complaints about such things were not generally tolerated. Nevertheless, Mom often sweetened the pot by offering to tell us a story while we were drying the dishes or churning butter for her. This was always a good deal because Mom was an excellent storyteller. We would focus on her story and hardly notice that we were simultaneously completing a chore. Mom made up the stories on the spot, and they always seemed to last until the chore was done.

One of the recurring characters in Mom's stories was an imaginary fellow named "Mo" and the stories always involved his faithful dog, "Hound Dog." We liked the stories so much that we frequently pestered Mom to tell us a "Mo and Hound Dog" story. Mom wisely saved the stories for those occasions when she needed us to help with some chore.

Mom's "Mo and Hound Dog" stories were always interesting and involved some aspect of country life we could identify with. I can only remember a few vignettes from some of the stories now, and I always wished Mom had written some of them down so we could have preserved them.

In one story we found amusing, Hound Dog kept running out of the house when Mo was trying to light a fire in the fireplace. Hound Dog couldn't be convinced that Mo wasn't trying to burn their cabin down. In another story, Hound Dog's friend, a white rabbit, managed to avoid a hunter by tip-toeing down the middle of the Shasta River with just the tip of his nose above water. Mom's stories were often funny, sometimes instructional and always managed to capture our imaginations. I don't know if a generation raised on television would appreciate stories like "Mo and Hound Dog," but they sure worked for us, before television – at the end of a dirt road.

FROM RADIO TO TELEVISION

In the years before we had television, the radio was our main
window on the world and a chief source of entertainment.
It was common for everybody to gather around and listen
to radio adventure stories in the evening the way families
gather around the television set today. "The Lone Ranger"
was a favorite, but there were other radio programs we
liked: "Captain Star," "Rin Tin Tin," "The Green Hornet,"
"The Shadow," "My Little Margie," "Our Miss Brooks" and
"Sergeant Preston of the Yukon."

On weekends there were daytime radio shows we would
listen to as we did our chores. There was the "Breakfast
Club," a variety show featuring interviews and singers. I
recall my amazement when I heard a singer who was just
about my age performing on the "Breakfast Club." Her
name was Brenda Lee, and she was a little girl with a great
big voice. "Big John and Sparkie" was our favorite children's show. On Sundays there was the "Comic Weekly
Man," who would read the newspaper comics to us. "The
Siskiyou Daily News" was our local newspaper, but it didn't
have the expanded comic section that we called the "funny
papers." The local paper was all in black and white and
had a rather limited comic section, so the "Comic Weekly
Man" allowed us to hear the funny papers even though we
couldn't see them.

The radio was often on during the day, and we got our news
and heard the latest songs over the radio. For the most part
we kids didn't pay too much attention to the radio unless
there was a comedy or adventure program on.

On weekends it seemed there was always a baseball game
on the radio. If there wasn't a professional team playing, the
local station would broadcast the Yreka City team's game.
I never did like baseball; there was nothing more boring

to me than listening to one. Baseball games seemed to be hopelessly slow-moving and endless. Just walking through a room where a baseball game was on the radio made me sleepy. Nobody in our family followed the sport or cared who won a game, and I couldn't imagine why anybody would ever pay money to go to a baseball game. In the early days we didn't have many radio station options in Siskiyou County, and once the baseball game came on KSYC you might as well turn it off. You were going to be bored to pieces if you left it on.

On Friday nights, the radio always broadcast the "Friday Night Fights." This was a live narrative description of professional boxing matches, or prizefights, as they were called. If Dad was home, he always listened intently to the prizefights, and we had to be real quiet so he could concentrate on the rapid-fire narrative description of the fights: *"A right to the jaw of Marciano, Marciano returns with two quick left jabs. Patterson ducks and returns a solid right to the head of Marciano. Marciano's hurt. Patterson lands two more jabs to the stomach and a right to Marciano's jaw. Marciano's down....."*

Dad listened to this while sitting on the edge of his favorite chair. If one of us kids made a slight noise or asked a question, we were told to be quiet in no uncertain terms. I found that the safest thing to do was to leave the room during the fights because it just wasn't possible to be quiet enough.

By the time I was in high school we had television on the ranch. I thought this was some kind of miracle – to sit in the living room on the ranch and watch a television program. We received two stations. Channel 7, out of Redding, was relatively clear, but Channel 12, out of Chico, was quite fuzzy. In those days almost everybody had a black-and-white television set, and relatively few programs were even broadcast in color. Whenever a program was going to be broadcast in color, it was a big deal and the TV station would show an animation of a peacock opening its tail like a fan (displaying a broad spectrum of colors which we saw in black and white) and announce, "The following program is brought to you in living color." We didn't have a color television on the ranch until I was in college.

Having a television set complicated our lives somewhat. Now we had to try to milk the cows after the cartoons but before Disney came on. It was always a disappointment when you had to leave in the middle of an interesting program to irrigate or do other chores.

On weekends, there were football games, and these were more interesting to watch than baseball or prizefights. My older brother Tom was a big football fan and played football in high school and later in college. Tom usually required me to watch football games with him. He was superior in size, and that left me with few options. I usually didn't mind watching football with Tom, but there was a ritual to follow. We had to pick opposite teams and root for our respective team during the game. We didn't really follow any particular team or care who won, but it was always nice to see a close game. Rooting for a particular team made it more interesting and fulfilled our basic need to compete against each other, even if only as spectators.

Picking a team wasn't difficult; your option was to pick the black team or the white team. Since we had a black-and-white TV, the teams' jerseys appeared to be either black or white, so you would pick one or the other. Whoever picked his team first determined who the other would have to root for. For instance, if Tom was the first to say, "Dibs on the black team," then I was stuck with the white team. The rules were simple, and the objective was to ensure that for each game there was a clear winner and loser. If your team won the game, you were entitled to jeer the loser and feel superior for the rest of the day. You had demonstrated the ability to pick the best team, so your superiority was evident for all to see.

HIRED HANDS

Through the years my father employed a variety of "hired hands" to help out around the ranch. Hired hands were particularly helpful in the early days, before Tom and I were old enough to help with ranch chores and again after we kids grew up and left the ranch. Ranch hired hands tend to be interesting people, some more interesting than others. They usually don't get paid well, but there are benefits like room and board, and fishing and hunting rights that help to make up the difference. Most hired hand types are deeply motivated by hunting and fishing opportunities.

Hired hands came with different skill levels and different levels of motivation. A hired hand with a basic skill set worthy of his pay was reasonably good at working unsupervised, knew something about animals, and could repair and maintain vehicles, farm equipment and fences. They knew or quickly learned how to do the routine chores such as irrigating during the summer and feeding cattle on the range during the winter. Dad made sure they were mending fences, chopping weeds or checking on the cattle when they didn't have anything else to do. On a ranch, when you don't have anything else to do, there's always something else to do.

Most of the hired hands we had on the ranch tended to be transient. Few of them stayed very long. I suspect that this was due in part to the type of personality that gravitates to that line of work. Some people seem to like a footloose life style, but the low pay and my father's hot temper undoubtedly had a lot to do with the brief duration of the stay for many of them.

Jess was one of the first hired hands I can remember. While working for my father, he slept in a one-room bunkhouse near the Red House and ate some of his meals with us. Like most of the hired hands, he was single and seemed to be hiding out from life. He liked to hunt and would sometimes kill a cottontail rabbit that we would have for dinner.

Like many of the hired hands, Jess was pretty close to being a real cowboy, and he taught my mother how to cook an authentic cowboy meal he said used to be served along the trail on cattle drives. It was officially called "(Expletive deleted) in a Sack," but Mom decided to call it something else. I don't remember everything that went into it, but, as I recall, it was essentially dried fruit added to a partially full sack of flour. When everything was inside the sack, a knot was tied at the end, and the whole thing was thrown into a pot of boiling water. I don't know how authentic that cowboy meal was, but I seriously doubt that it was served up on cattle drives. Not only did it taste lousy, but it gave you so much gas you would run a serious risk of spooking the cattle into a stampede.

Jess taught Tom and me to eat pickled pigs' feet. They came in a jar, and all three of us sat around his bunkhouse eating out of the jar. Pigs' feet didn't taste too bad if you didn't think about what you were eating and didn't make the mistake of actually looking at them. We liked to visit Jess in the bunkhouse because he was friendly, entertaining and he collected unusual things. We were particularly interested in his ashtray, which looked like a coiled rattlesnake. My mother encouraged us to stay away from the bunkhouse, but I never could figure if she was trying to protect us from Jess, or Jess from us.

One of the hired hands – it might have been Jess – drove Tom and me into Yreka to see a movie once. It was a rare treat to get to see a movie, so we were glad to have the opportunity to go. The movie title was something like "Superman and the Mole-Men." In terms of quality, it was whatever comes more than a few pegs below B-grade, but we didn't care. This was many years before television, and we weren't about to be picky about *any* movie.

Sometimes a hired hand would just up and disappear. He'd get a paycheck and never be seen again. I remember my father would come home from work to find out that yet another hired hand was gone, so Dad had to go out and do the man's work until he found another one. One hired hand announced that he had just received a letter from his wife, who said she would take him back again. He collected his final check and was gone that same day. On another occasion a hired hand simply vanished without a word, leaving his belongings (such as they were) behind. My father suspected the law was after him.

It was difficult to find and keep a reliable hired hand, and very few stayed more than a season or a few months. The ones who did stay were generally reliable and well worth their pay. The hunting and fishing fringe benefits helped to make up for the low pay, and some people just appreciate being able to live and work in the country.

The succession of hired-hand characters that came through the ranch was part of what made life interesting. Even as a little boy I could tell that some of the men my father hired were a few megahertz off frequency, but, when you need help and can't afford to pay much, you can't always be choosy. When my father was getting old and was living alone on the ranch, he again had to hire men to help him out. The pay was still low, but the fringe benefits included a house or trailer to live in, hunting and fishing, a side of beef every year and the ability to work alone in the rugged beauty of Siskiyou County. We later found evidence that some of these hired hands had supplemented their income by growing pot down on the river. Times change at the end of a dirt road – but people don't.

A DISTINGUISHED VISITOR

In the 1960s a special guest visited the ranch. The guest was an actor, not one of particular renown, but nevertheless a "real" movie actor. I was home from college at the time, and it was exciting to think that we were going have a visitor of some prominence. After all, the ranch was not normally a stopover for famous people.

The actor turned out to be down-home friendly – a regular guy. He was easy to talk with, and while he stayed with us we shared a steak dinner, and he went for a walk down by the lake. We talked about many things, including politics and his experiences as an actor. He happened to be on the road campaigning for a politician and stayed at our ranch for a bit of rest and relaxation between speaking engagements in Siskiyou County.

My mother was active in the Siskiyou County Republican's Women organization, and that's how we ended up hosting the actor at the ranch. It never entered our minds that the man sitting at our table would one day become governor of California and then President of the United States.

In the 1960s Ronald Reagan was emerging into national politics by campaigning for Barry Goldwater. Reagan struck me as a man with strong convictions and a willingness to act on them. I think the record will reflect that my initial impressions were correct. The future President Reagan's visit was a brush with greatness; he was no doubt the most famous visitor we hosted at the end of a dirt road.

THIS GATE SEPARATES FIELD NO. 3 FROM NO. 4 ON THE ROAD FROM THE RED HOUSE TO THE RIVER. IN THE LATE AFTERNOON SUN, IT'S A GATE TO MANY RANCH MEMORIES.

CHAPTER SIXTEEN

WHEN THE DUST SETTLES

As each of the four Nelson sons grew up, he left the ranch at the end of a dirt road to find his place in the world. Tom, the oldest, was the first to leave for college, in 1960. He eventually became self-employed as an appraiser and settled with his family in the State of Washington. I was next to head off for college, in 1962. Dave followed a few years after me; he ended up in sales and eventually settled in South Lake Tahoe, California.

It was Dan's misfortune to be the last one out the door. He had to experience first-hand the acrimonious divorce of our parents. All of us got to share some of the pain and anger of the divorce, but he had to live with it on a daily basis. Dan eventually got a doctorate in soil science (we call him "Dan, the Dirt Doctor") and settled in Moses Lake, Washington, where he runs his own business, called Soiltest Farm Consultants, Inc. Tom and Dan married sisters – fewer in-laws to break in that way.

While attending college, all of us returned to the ranch from time to time to visit or to work through the summer, but once you leave home, you never come back the same person you were when you left. When you leave home, you become part of a larger world. Your new world includes new friends and family, as well as new commitments, responsibilities, ideas, experiences and perspectives. Once you leave home, you can never come back to who you were or the way it was.

In high school my life began to change in significant ways. One noteworthy experience was learning to play the guitar. My mother had given me piano lessons when I was much younger, but I was not interested in music or the piano, and resisted both the lessons and mandatory practicing.

I can still see my piano teacher sitting on the bench next to me, resting her exasperated forehead on her arm, which was braced against the piano. She would point to the sheet music and ask, "What's this note?"

I seldom knew what the heck note it was and was making no serious effort to learn. I would make a wild guess and hit a key on the piano, **PLUNK.** "Is it this one?"

"No," the teacher shook her head slowly.

PLINK. "Is it this one?"

"No," still shaking her head.

PLING. "Is it this one?"

Finally by accident or lucky guess, I would find the correct note or, better yet, the teacher would show me the note by hitting it for me. I learned new tunes by memorizing the notes by their positions on the piano keyboard. Sometimes I recognized the right note on the sheet music, sometimes I found the note by accident and much of the time the teacher would show me which note to play. I just memorized what she showed me and learned to play a few tunes by imitation.

The sheet music in front of me was little more than window dressing. Eventually my stubbornness paid off, and I won the piano wars. My mother surrendered unconditionally, and the lessons came to an end.

My interest in the guitar began unexpectedly prior to high school while listening to my brother's Kingston Trio records. I spent hours listening to Tom's records and eventually began singing along with them. Soon I found myself playing air guitar along with them – as the fourth member of the Kingston Quartet. While I never could sing very well, I got pretty good at air guitar. Encouraged by this initial success, I migrated from air guitar to strumming a tennis racket and found I could play "Tom Dooley" as well as the Kingston Trio. Inspired by my obvious talent and quick mastery of the air and tennis racket instruments, I decided I'd like to try to play a real guitar – it couldn't be that difficult.

During the time my interest in guitar picking was developing, Elmo Smith, a local banker and a family friend, was a frequent visitor to the ranch. As luck would have it, he was once a professional musician and excellent guitarist. To my delight, he often brought a guitar out to the ranch and played beautiful music for us. I watched his hands intently to see how he did it. He made it look so easy. Elmo noticed my interest in the guitar and volunteered to show me a few chords to get me started. That's when I learned that I had apparently been born with my hands on backwards. Elmo would demonstrate the correct finger position for a particular chord, and I would contort my fingers in a hopeless attempt to duplicate his. The guitar had six strings and I only had five fingers; it seemed almost an impossible task, not nearly as easy or as intuitive as air or tennis racket guitar.

I didn't even own a guitar when I first began to learn a few chords, so Elmo loaned me his old rosewood Martin guitar. Today I own two Martin guitars and realize that Elmo's would be worth several thousand dollars today. I laid down my faithful air guitar and began practicing regularly with that old rosewood Martin, while dreams of becoming a rock-and-roll king stirred my imagination. My musical interests had drifted away from the Kingston Trio and folk music, and I was inspired by a popular guitar instrumental group called the Ventures. I bought two of their records and practiced regularly, hoping one day to be able to play just like them.

Now that I was pursuing a musical interest of my own, my mother didn't have to remind me to practice. I practiced on a daily basis, driven by my own interests and ambition. In fact, on more than one occasion my mother came into my room after midnight to tell me, "Put that thing away; you're going to wake everybody up." That was a switch, I thought, now she's encouraging me *not* to practice!

While I was learning to play the guitar I pestered everyone I encountered who knew anything about guitars. I tried to get them to show me something new. This was as close to guitar lessons as I came. I really wanted to master the guitar, so I picked the brains and talents of others as much as I picked Elmo's Martin. When someone would show me a new tune, lick or chord, I would go home and practice it until I had it down.

Soon after I entered high school, I ordered a Silvertone electric guitar out of a Sears catalogue and joined with some other high school friends to form a band we called Mike and the Midnighters. Mike was the drummer and most talented member of the group. Duncan played the saxophone, and he was the next most accomplished musician. Buck was next on the descending talent scale, and he played lead guitar. Then there was me, former air guitar and tennis racket virtuoso, playing rhythm guitar. I may have been the bottom guy on the talent totem pole, but I was a member of the band and that's what mattered to me. In the early 1960s, two guitars, a saxophone and a drummer made a fairly typical teen dance band. Mike and the Midnighters played at teen dances around the county and actually made some money. It was a fun time.

If anyone ever accused me of being a musician, there wouldn't be enough evidence to convict me. I have never been a really proficient guitar player, but it has remained part of my life. In high school it was Mike and the Midnighters with rock and roll, and in college it was The Smokey Finger Boys with country music. As an adult I played for a time with Gospel Creek, a Christian bluegrass band.

Although I enjoyed my status and regional fame as a teenage rock-and-roller, I was preoccupied by conflicting thoughts and feelings as my turn to leave the ranch approached. By the time I was in high school, I knew my departure was coming, but I had mixed feelings. Part of me wanted to stay a kid on the ranch and part of me wanted to bust out into the adult world. It was an awkward time – sometimes I would go for a hike just to get away to a quiet place to try to sort things out. I felt unprepared to face a world that I knew would be drastically different from my life at the end of a dirt road.

My ambivalence increased as the date of my graduation approached. I saw graduation from high school as the first step into adult life. I had watched my older brother Tom leave for college, but he seemed so much more mature and capable than I was. I knew my parents expected me to go to college, and I wanted to go, but I worried that I would disappoint them and humiliate myself by flunking out. I had little confidence and no idea what I wanted to be when I grew up. How could I ever decide on a course of study in college? I couldn't even decide which college to attend.

Through high school my brothers and I had summer jobs to earn money for college. Tom was a big, tough football type, so he made good money bucking bales and hauling hay for various contractors in the county. It was hard work, but it kept him in good shape for football. I was smaller and not the hay-hauling type, so, with my father's help, I managed to land a job working at the Siskiyou County fairgrounds.

Mr. Matthews, the fair manager, hired me, but my immediate boss was a man by the name of Russ Whitlock. Russ was a gnarly older fellow who looked, dressed, walked and talked the way I imagined a real cowboy would. He went by the name of "Slim," and he worked us hard. He wasn't hesitant to tell us when we did a bad job, but he would also compliment us when we did a good one. We always knew where we stood with Slim. I worked by myself or sometimes with Slim's son, Steve, or with Ross, a friend from high school. We did everything from hoeing weeds to watering flowers, sweeping floors, hauling and spreading sawdust, helping with construction projects, mowing lawns, and putting up and taking down fair decorations. Whatever needed to be done, we did it. I even had the opportunity to paint a small mural in the flower display shed, the first and only time I was paid for my artwork.

After working at the fairgrounds for several years, I managed to get a better paying job with Pacific Power and Light (PP&L), which was the southern Oregon and northern California counterpart of Pacific Gas & Electric. My job with PP&L (today called Pacific Power) lasted through most of my college years. I worked at Iron Gate Reservoir, which was about a 25-mile drive north of the ranch. My job consisted of maintenance and odd jobs such as cleaning the picnic and camping facilities at the reservoir. It was an outside job, and I got to interact with the public quite a bit. I also got to go inside the Iron Gate Dam on a regular basis. This was always an interesting experience as it was filled with huge turbines, pipes and gauges. It was also extremely noisy as the large water-driven turbines spun to generate electricity.

Choosing a college to attend was determined when I received a letter from the Sacramento State College (now California State University, Sacramento) gymnastics coach. He invited me to come to Sac State to join the gymnastics team. I was active on the Yreka High School gymnastics team, and the Sac State gymnastics coach had been to Yreka and seen me perform. His invitation was gratifying and was the final factor in determining where I would attend college. I wasn't offered a scholarship, but I was offered assistance in obtaining a job if I needed one. Now, at least I knew where I wanted to go to college.

My ambivalence was running rampant when the day came to leave for college. The kid in me was insecure and wanted to stay on the ranch; the young adult in me wanted to embark on a new adventure. I was leaving friends, family and a girlfriend behind, but I was going to meet my future. I felt unprepared but knew it was my time to go. Was I going to flunk out of college? Would I fail to qualify for the gymnastics team? Would I be able to deal with city life? There was a sea of uncertainty ahead of me as Mom drove me out the dirt road and turned west on A-12.

Upon arriving in Sacramento we found the on-campus dormitories were already full, so I obtained a list of available off-campus housing for students. Within a few hours we found a boarding house on H Street a few miles from campus. I placed all my belongings in my room – which was slightly larger than a closet – and Mom took me out for an early dinner. After dinner, she dropped me off in front of the boarding house, and we said our goodbyes, both of us with obviously large lumps in our throat. There was no hug or kiss goodbye, but that was par for the course – Nelsons didn't hug and kiss, we just mumbled goodbye or good luck and maybe shook hands. As Mom drove away I stood alone on the Sacramento sidewalk, the lump in my throat refusing to go away. There was still ranch dust on my shoes, but after a 250-mile drive, the ranch seemed at least a million miles away.

That goodbye was the worst of it. It was difficult adjusting to living in a boarding house, getting used to living in a city and adapting to college routines, but soon enough these things became familiar and even friendly to me. Another difficult adjustment for me was trading a view that stretched to the horizon for a view of the house across the street. Sacramento was geographically flat and visually cramped. I missed my hills and open vistas.

Within a few weeks of my arrival at college, Sara, my high school girlfriend, sent me a "Dear John" letter. This took the wind out of my sails for a few weeks, but, like so many things in life that seem so tragic at the time, it was best for both of us. For one thing, it cleared my social calendar for Valerie (not the Valerie I stuck my tongue out at Big Springs School), who would be the real love of my life.

College life was ever so different from my life at the end of a dirt road. My studies and gymnastics schedule kept me busy most of the time. I attended a First Covenant church and participated in their college-age youth group. I made new friends at church as well as on campus. Eventually I was able to move into Draper Hall on campus, where I roomed with Mike Jones, a friend from Yreka High School back in Siskiyou County. Mike had a car and gave me rides home with him during Christmas and semester breaks.

Mike and I both played the guitar, and we had a good time picking and strumming together. Sometimes other residents of Draper Hall would drop by our room to listen to us, and other times they would drop by to tell us to shut up so they could study. Bob Summerville, a younger resident of Draper Hall with a good singing voice and a banjo, heard Mike and I playing and joined our "band." Bob came from a chicken ranch near Susanville, which he referred to as the "Chickarosa." Our music tended toward country at the time, but we mixed in a little folk and came close to blue-grass with a few tunes.

We formed an informal band, which we called the Smokey Finger Boys – a play on words based on a real band called the Smokey Mountain Boys. What the Smokey Finger Boys lacked in virtuosity, we made up with volume, and all except those trying to study in the vicinity had a good time.

While in college I returned to the ranch each summer to work for PP&L at Iron Gate. The ranch was no longer my home in the way it was before. It was still home, but it was really the place I stayed when I wasn't at school. Things were changing. While at home I attended the Yreka Berean Church regularly. When I was a junior in high school my girlfriend, Sara, had invited me to attend church with her, and I had become a Christian. This was a turning point in my life. My relationship with Sara was temporal, but my relationship with the Lord is eternal. Between college and church I was maturing in spiritual as well as intellectual directions. I wasn't there yet (and I'm still not), but I was growing and changing.

The Nelson family didn't attend church. My father was a self-described agnostic, and my mother was a religious eclectic, subscribing to various non-traditional doctrines, most of which would be considered cultic by biblical standards. In any event, I was the only Nelson attending church at the time. My mother remained a bit distant to my faith because it differed so much from her beliefs, and my father treated my faith with the same enthusiasm he exhibited when, as a child, I learned to color between the lines in my coloring book. He seemed to be saying in a condescending way, "Good for you," while hoping I would grow out of it. Both parents encouraged me "not to overdo it" when it came to religion.

I was home on summer break between my freshman and sophomore years at college when I had my first date with Valerie, the girl I would one day marry. The circumstances of our first date could, at best, be described as unusual. I had met Valerie at church but decided she was interested in another guy, so I put her off limits in my mind. I was not about to enter into a competition for this maiden – not because she wasn't worth it, but because I had no confidence that anyone that wonderful could fall for me.

In the meantime, I had a longstanding but distant interest in Millie, the daughter of a Big Springs rancher who was a friend of the Nelson family. I managed to muster up enough courage to call Millie on the phone and invited her to attend the Siskiyou County Fair with me. The fair was located in Yreka and was a good place for a date because there was plenty to do: a carnival, a rodeo, stage entertainment, lots of animals, and a wide variety of commercial, agricultural and food booths. She agreed, and we arranged to meet at the Big Springs booth at a particular time.

At the appointed time, I showed up at the Big Springs 4-H Booth and waited for Millie to arrive for our date. She never showed up. I waited for over an hour and a half and finally gave up. I was feeling dejected and rejected, and began walking aimlessly, oblivious to the music and bright lights of the fair. While on this journey to nowhere in particular, I chanced to encounter Miss Valerie Grey in the company of Lou and Becky Coles, an elderly couple with whom Valerie was living in town. Valerie was from Happy Camp, some 40 miles down the Klamath River from Yreka. It was a small town with a big reputation as an isolated community where strange people lived and bizarre things – like Big Foot sightings – happened. Happy Camp wasn't the end of the earth, but people said you could see it from there. Valerie's family was far more dysfunctional (a term I didn't learn for another 20 years) than mine, but she was still a "Happy Camper."

The Coles, Valerie and I all went to the same church and knew each other, so we began to walk and talk together. Finally Becky Coles (that sweet, scheming little old lady from Prince Edward Island) said in her Canadian accent, "Chuck, it's getting late, and Lou and I are getting tired, would you mind terribly taking Valerie home tonight?" Those were the sweetest words I could have heard. All of us knew what Becky was up to, and everybody was ever so glad to go along with it. That was my first date with Valerie. We skipped the carnival and just walked and talked, visited the animals then sat and talked some more.

At one point Valerie and I passed Millie, who was walking the other way. She had a cowboy on either side of her, and while our eyes met, we didn't say anything to each other. I thought I had been stood up for the two cowboys, and she figured she had been stood up for another girl. We were both wrong.

The next day my mother received a call from Millie's mother inquiring why I had failed to meet up with her daughter. It turned out that while Millie and I had agreed to meet at the Big Springs "booth" when we had talked on the phone, we had failed to communicate. By the Big Springs booth I had meant the Big Springs 4-H booth and Millie had meant the Big Springs concession booth, where hamburgers, hot dogs and sodas were sold. We had each showed up at the appointed time but at different locations. The mix-up was simple miscommunication, but I have come to believe that, in the grand scheme of things, it was no accident.

Valerie and I were married during my final semester of college. In June of 1966, on the Monday morning following graduation from college in Sacramento, I enrolled at the Oakland Police Department recruit academy in Oakland, California. Without ever considering a career in law enforcement while growing up, I ended up majoring in public administration with a specialization in police administration. I had taken an exploratory course in criminal law prior to declaring a major and got hooked on law and law enforcement. With encouragement from my boss while I worked part-time as a student professional assistant in the law enforcement branch of the California Division of Forestry, I had applied to the Oakland Police Department because it had a good reputation and provided opportunities for advancement.

While my transition from ranch living to city living began in Sacramento, I was unprepared for the stark differences between rural ranching and municipal law enforcement. A law enforcement career tends to generate a major paradigm shift in anyone; it's just a bit bigger when the transition is from milking cows to catching bank robbers.

A few years later, when I was a beat cop in downtown Oakland, I was having a desperately needed cup of coffee in an all-night café around 4:00 in the morning. I was surrounded by Oakland's "night critters" and carrying on a casual conversation with a drag queen. As I took in where I was and what I was doing, it struck me that I was a long way geographically and culturally from Siskiyou County, the Yreka Berean Church and the ranch where I grew up.

While my law enforcement career was winding up in the city, my parents' marriage was winding down on the ranch. After more than 30 years of marriage, when they should have been enjoying the fruits of their labor, their relationship was coming apart. It seems that after most of the kids had left the nest, my parents looked at each other across the table and realized that they didn't have anything in common apart from children, a tragic error made by many couples.

After the divorce my father stayed on the ranch, and my mother purchased a 13-acre farm near Oregon House, California. When the farm became too much for her to handle, she moved into a small condominium in Modesto, California.

During my 34-year law enforcement career, I noticed an interesting thing happening in me. While I had no interest in becoming a rancher, my appreciation for the experiences I had growing up on a ranch increased. I have been a big city cop, an FBI agent and a transit district police officer, but I always saw myself as a country boy working in the city. I was living in the city, but my roots were still embedded in the ranch. I was living out the expression, "You can take the boy out of the country, but you can't take the country out of the boy."

My visits to the ranch took on a new importance. The stresses that built up in me in the course of my difficult law enforcement career would dissipate when I returned to the ranch. It was as if my stress load was an electric charge bleeding away when a circuit becomes grounded. The ranch was my "ground" in more ways than one, and all I had to do was walk on it to discharge my accumulated stress.

With the occasional visit to the ranch to reset my psyche, I could return refreshed and energized to the world of suspects, victims, witnesses and night critters. I could deal with the sights, sounds and dangers of a career in law enforcement and work within a system of justice where justice seemed so often thwarted, as long as I could occasionally remind myself that there was another world beyond the city limits. No doubt my visits to the ranch took me back to a childhood where life was simpler, but, more important, it reminded me that there was more to life than bureaucracy and crime in the city. There was also fresh air, bronco grass and birds; and the sights, sounds and smells of creation. These creations of God directed my thoughts to the God of creation and gave me the perspective I needed to cope with what came my way in the line of duty.

The Nelson Ranch played different roles in the lives of each member of the Nelson family. At one time it was a dream come true for my parents. It remained the center of my father's dreams, but it became a place of bitter memories for my mother. When we moved onto the ranch, I can remember my mother singing as she worked around the house. She had a beautiful voice, and it seemed she sang her way through the day. Somewhere along the way she lost the song in her heart, and by the time I was in high school I never heard my mother sing.

The ranch was where all the Nelson boys grew up, but each one of us experienced it in a different way. We each grew up in the same house but in slightly different homes. I can't speak for my brothers, but the ranch was my home as a boy and my "ground" or "centering place" as an adult. In a way that I am unable to explain rationally, the ranch parented me – it was my comfort, my escape, my place of peace.

After retirement, I visited the ranch as often as I could to soak up its comforts and to prepare myself to say goodbye. Joint ownership among brothers with different lives and needs was not an ideal arrangement. I knew the day was coming when the ranch I loved would have to be sold.

The dust of Nelson Road settled for the last time behind my father in December of 1991. He had lived alone on the ranch during the last years of his life. I don't think this was as sad to him as it seems to me. He loved the ranch more than he loved anything and perhaps anybody else, but his unbridled anger had ensured his solitude in his final years. He was the product of a broken and dysfunctional home, and it played itself out in his life. He did the best he could with what he had – given his unwillingness to seek help beyond himself.

Shortly after my father died, my mother stayed at the ranch for a few days, but it was a difficult experience for her. She was haunted by the bad memories of a thorny marriage and a bitter divorce. She had endured the marriage for the sake of her children but was unable to rekindle her love for the ranch that was once everything she wanted. After a few short days she left the ranch with no desire to return and died in her Modesto home in August of 2001.

The day finally came when the last Nelson drove out Nelson Road and turned east on the paved county road. The dust finally settled over 50 years of laughter, labor, dreams, joys and heartaches – all the stuff of life lived on what was the Nelson Ranch. I may be physically absent from the ranch now, but, as long as I live, my memories will continue to soar like a thousand eagles over the rocks, between the hills, beside the lake and along the river. You can take the boy out of the country, but you will never take the country out of the man he became. I will still hear the sounds, savor the smells and remember. The sale of the ranch was a sad day for me. But I find some solace in knowing the coyotes will still howl, the killdeer and meadowlarks will still sing, and a certain fish that once had my name on it will survive to spawn again – on the ranch at the end of a dirt road.

THE SUN SETS ON THE SHASTA RIVER – ON THE RANCH AT THE END OF A DIRT ROAD.

EPILOGUE

In June of 2005, the Nelson Ranch was acquired by The Nature Conservancy through Stillwater Ranches. Thanks to the efforts of these conservation-minded organizations, the ranch at the end of a dirt road, with its rich history and vital natural resources, will be preserved into the future.

A RANCHER'S WORK IS NEVER DONE

Well, here's another day. The sun's not even up yet, and that dad-burned rooster's been crowing for an hour. But it don't matter, the house smells of fresh perked coffee, and I got a hot steaming cup in my hand while I sit for a spell. Ol' Shep's chin's on my knee, and he's watching me real close, hoping I might drop something he can eat. But he's always ready to go when I am.

This morning I better fix the tractor so I can work on the ditch out by the alfalfa field. It's starting to leak again. If the leak wets the field before I rake the hay, I won't be able to get to it before next week, and I'll be way behind schedule again. Guess I better fix the fence in the North 40 where that Hereford bull took it down before he went lame. That reminds me, I better call the vet today. Dang, there goes another $200 down the drain. I sure hope the pickup starts; it's been running real rough and needs some work. Maybe I can get to that after I shoe the horse, which reminds me, we're almost out of grain. Guess I better pick some up next time I'm in town.

That old barn sure could use a paint job; you can hardly tell it once was red. I really can't afford the paint or the time now 'cause I better fix that roof first before the hay gets wet next time it rains. I guess that can wait though. I'll have to fix the gate at the corral before next Tuesday if we're gonna get the cattle shipped on time. That reminds me, I better get some help lined up for Tuesday. Guess I'll call somebody today if the phone's working. Gotta get that thing fixed one of these days.

Boy! The wife is gonna get cross if I don't repair the hole in the screen door that's been letting all the flies into the house. Guess I better get some screen next time I go in to town.

I sure hope the pump doesn't break down again 'cause I gotta start irrigating the South 60 by the day after tomorrow. I'm gonna have to work on that pump some, which reminds me, I better spray the weeds along the ditch before I start irrigating. Those yellow-star and bull thistles are really getting out of hand. I wonder where I left that sprayer last. I think I still have some spray, but if I don't, I can pick some up next time I'm in town – if the pickup will start.

Boy! The price of fertilizer is sure getting up there. Wish I could just raise my prices whenever I want to cover my expenses. Oh well, it don't matter, it's starting to get light now. Guess I'll go out to the shop and fix that wrench I broke last week, so I can get to work on the tractor. Darn, the coffee pot's getting cold, looks like the element's gone out again. I'm gonna have to fix that thing one of these days. C'mon, Shep, let's go. Sun's almost up. Atta boy!

APPENDIX B

A SISKIYOU SUMMER DAY

The cool of the morning is soon blown away
By the heat of the sun on a midsummer's day

The dew of the night is quickly swept from the ground
Sipped by the sun while making its rounds

The valley is rimmed by blue mountains tall
With Mt. Shasta its centerpiece, the grandest of all

The grass on the hills in the valley below
Has long lost its green to the sun's summer glow

Bronco grass nods as a breeze passes by
Chased by the heat that comes from the sky

Winds hit the blue mountains and climb without stop
Then leap to the sky to form clouds without tops

The sun and the wind and the mountains together
Are working in concert to bring change to the weather

Clouds billow above the blue mountains below
Then join hands together and march to and fro

The hot sun is blocked and the scene is a wonder
For there's a bow in the sky and faraway thunder

It's a beauty to see and many will say
There's nothing that beats a Siskiyou summer day

APPENDIX C

KISSED BY THE SKY

While hiking on a hot summer day, a dark shadow unexpectedly overtakes you, lifting the heat of the sun from your shoulders. A puff of wind blows gently across the sweat on your brow. Your heart leaps as a sudden clap of thunder splits the air above your head. Its awesome power vibrates deep into your chest as it rumbles through the clouds and bounces from hill to hill around you. The birds are suddenly silent.

A small something hits the ground behind you. Another one lands to your side. An ice-cold raindrop finds a patch of bare skin on the back of your neck. It's so cold that for an instant it feels like a hot coal pressed against your skin. Soon your ears are filled with the *pit pat patter* of larger drops of rain as they hit the ground around you. The smell of ozone reaches your nose and, almost reflexively, you inhale deeply, savoring the cool refreshing smells of summer rain.

The bronco grass bows deeply as a gust of chilled wind brushes past you, pushing a tumbleweed ahead of it. The gust twists into a small whirlwind, tossing dry grass into the air as it moves away. Now silver drops streak past your eyes, and the sounds and smells of a summer thundershower fill your senses. Dark fingers of rain arch down from the clouds overhead, and the soft rumble of distant thunder reaches your ears as grumbling clouds continue on their way. The summer's heat is gone, and the hairs on your arm stand straight up as a shiver ripples down your back.

The thundershower is over as quickly as it came. The sun falls bright on your eyes and hot on your skin as it emerges from behind the clouds. The birds resume singing. As you watch the rain shadow moving away across the dry hills, you realize that your hike has produced an unexpected reward. You have been kissed by the sky.

LIFE AT THE END OF A DIRT ROAD
PHOTOS FROM NELSON FAMILY ALBUM

ACCORDING TO TOM, THIS IS THE OCCASION HE SAVED MY LIFE BY ADMINISTERING THE HEIMLICH MANEUVER (EST. 1946)

SEDG, CHUCK, TOM. (EST. 1948)

CHUCK & TOM SHORTLY AFTER MOVING ONTO THE RANCH. (EST. 1948)

JESS (THE FIRST HIRED HAND), TOM, SEDG, CHUCK & SHEP. (EST 1949)

LEFT:
TOM, LIGHTNING
CHUCK. (EST. 1949)

RIGHT:
SHEEP, CHUCK,
TOM. (EST. 1950).

TOM & CHUCK WITH THEIR NEW BABY BROTHER DAVID. (EST. 1950)

DAVID TAKES A
REST. (EST. 1950)

ELSIE & SEDG WITH GOLDIE
(NOT HER BEST SIDE) DAVID,
CHUCK & TOM – MOVING INTO
THE NEW HOUSE. (EST. 1952)

ELSIE & SEDG WITH DAN (NEW ARRIVAL),
DAVID, CHUCK & TOM. (EST. 1955)

TOM – CHUCK – DAVID: SCHOOL PICTURES. (EST. 1956)

CHUCK (EST. 1956)

DAN AND "JOE" (EST. 1957)

HAULING HAY FROM NO. 5 FIELD. (EST. 1957)

LEFT: CHUCK WITH IMPROVISED HAT. (EST. 1948)

RIGHT: SHEEP, SHEP & CHUCK. (EST. 1949)

LEFT: SHEEP, DAVE, CHUCK & TOM. (EST. 1951)

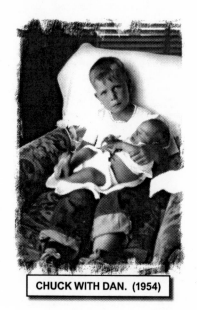

CHUCK WITH DAN. (1954)

DAVE, DAN, CHUCK, TOM. (1955)

DAVE, CHUCK, TOM. (EST. 1954-55)

LEFT: THE NELSON BOYS
– CHUCK, DAN, TOM &
DAVID. (EST. 1958)

RIGHT: THE NELSON
BOYS – TOM & CHUCK
[IN COLLEGE], DAVID
[HIGH SCHOOL] AND
DAN THE FUTURE
"DIRT DOCTOR"
[ELEMENTARY
SCHOOL]. (EST. 1964)

Breinigsville, PA USA
30 December 2009
229932BV00001B/6/A